Dreaming Synchronicity
Journey of an Empath

By Lyra Adams

Copyright © 2018 Lyra Adams
All rights reserved.

Book reviewers, booksellers, and librarians may quote brief passages and post cover image in a printed, online or broadcast review/notice without permission from the publisher. Otherwise, no part of this publication may be reproduced physically or digitally, stored in a retrieval system, or transmitted in any form or by any means (including electronic, mechanical, photocopying, recording or otherwise) without prior written permission from the publisher.

ISBN: 978-0-692-07521-0

Media info available at www.lyraadams.com

Life Garden Publishing Inc.

LIFE GARDEN
PUBLISHING INC

This book is dedicated to

All who are soft, yet resilient, in spirit

All those who wander

All those who wonder

All who desire to break free

Please visit **lyraadams.com** for her insightful blog, projects currently in the works and occasional free goodies.

Twitter: @lyraadams

Facebook: @authorlyraadams

Goodreads: goodreads.com/lyraadamsauthor

Table of Contents

A Letter To You 5
Beyond Coincidence 9
Hobos 13
Beginning 19
Leaving The Church 31
The Con Man 37
Endings and Beginnings 51
The Ambulance 63
A Sacrifice 67
The Magic of Unicorns 73
UFOs & A Little Help From My Friends 81
Miracle 91
The Voice 107
Facing My Ugly Monster 111
Healing 117
Skating On Thin Ice 127
Rebuilding Camelot 131
Dreams 141
Soul Mates 145
Alchemy in Action 153
Ripples 161
The Law of One 163
Bonds of Blood 171

An Interlude.. *175*
Loss of Control... *179*
Embryonic Darkness... *185*
Pluto's Punch.. *191*
Weaning.. *201*
The Living Nightmare.. *207*
Epilogue.. *213*

A Letter To You

Dear Reader,

In *Dreaming Synchronicity*, you will learn of deeply intimate and true experiences I have had with an invisible force that is not totally understood but experienced by many on a frequent basis.

There is a part of us that knows life is much larger than what we have been taught and our five senses perceive. Hidden, we glimpse it through occurrences which may seem enlightening or even alarming at times. This can come in the form of dreams, visions, strange coincidences and meetings. Often unusual in nature, these events can swing toward tragedy or the polar opposite of what we call miracles.

A lifetime on earth is short, even if you live to be a centenarian. Woven into each life will be a series of small, medium or large synchronicities. Chronicled herein are snapshot vignettes containing some of the most synchronistic events I have experienced, often laced with a strong dose of the supernatural. Dreams that are precognitive precede many of these moments.

Yet, this writing is about more than just synchronicities and the power of dreams. This memoir is about endings and beginnings. It is about psychology and metaphysical happenings. You may be triggered by the psychological, physical and sexual abuse contained inside this recounting.

Why am I sharing these intimate details of my life? I share this because I want you to know what is possible with synchronicity. Assuming you have experienced it many times yourself, it is always interesting to hear what others have had happen to them. This is also an opportunity for you to pause, think, and come to your own conclusions about fate, free will, coincidences, precognition and intuition.

Inviting you into my synchronistic life stories, you may find yourself feeling as if you are reading fiction at times. Everything is authentic without embellishment. Names have been changed and often, a first name is used only.

My point in this writing is not to convince you how synchronicity occurs. I have spent considerable time exploring the subject in detail and have clues, but no complete answers. I think this is an honest approach. In my research, I came across some who lend very valid glimpses into how synchronicity may happen. I found others who tried to make a case, but fell short for one reason or another. I do believe there is a trick of sorts to attracting more of it in your life.

My personal belief about synchronicity is that we share a field made up of threads that are energetic in nature. These threads weave a fabric that is interconnected with the threads of others, much like a spider web that binds everything together. A more poetic way to look at it is a tapestry. We are all in this tapestry together and God Source is the creator of the tapestry. We are all threads interacting and making up the picture. Only later, when we step back and look at the tapestry, we see that we had a story and it was made up of bits and pieces that if carefully listened to, followed and tended, would turn into a unique work of art with the signature of all of us joining as one.

Time, as we know it, does not exist in this artful energy field. Everything is there at once: the past, present and future. Yet, we only see momentary glimpses and experience that as our 'now'. Upon reflection, we see what we call our past. From this life experience on Earth and our individual perception, we are never aware of the complete picture that the tapestry contains.

Most of us have learned in psychology about the conscious, subconscious and super conscious portions of the mind. The super conscious could be related to the God Source field I speak of. Since time is irrelevant at this level, little bits of information leak through to our subconscious and conscious from it. These leaks may be the reason for humans experiencing déjà vu and premonitions.

Synchronicity is a series of events that are sometimes intuitive in nature. The overall theme is to examine these events from my own perspective which may, at times, bring out my own spiritual views. It should be noted that I have no desire to influence anyone's religion or spirituality. That is a choice of their free will. Yet, it does come out on the pages in my thoughts or reflections, simply because these experiences are mine.

Greater than any theme spoken of heretofore, this book reflects patterns and the tremendous effect they have on our lives. When I think of the why for this memoir, it is to know that it is possible to break free from human patterns that hold us in a type of slavery that we often have trouble seeing in ourselves. By listening to the stories of others, knowledge and understanding brings faster results toward human wholeness. Always, by looking at self primarily and analyzing our thoughts and patterns, we begin to see how we can break free and live a more harmonious life.

We are witnessing a generation of people who have grown up abused and some who continue to abuse in ways worse than most of us have ever imagined. They have learned this behavior and it can be unlearned. If they are not abusers and manipulators, they are often stuck in a victim role.

We are also witnessing record numbers of sex trafficking victims and this has become the number two pervasive crime in the United States, if not worldwide, right behind illegal drug distribution. It is possible to heal trauma from sexual abuse. It is possible to have a fulfilling sexual life after the trauma.

From this sharing, you will recognize archetypes and the nature of humankind falling easily into patterns that keep us on the same wheel continuously. Spinning around, we continue to experience things repetitively, either with the same or new people. We can feel tempted to say we are doomed and this is what life has dealt us until we reclaim our power by taking responsibility in our circumstances. Once we do this, our power that was previously subdued begins to produce something amazing for us in our life, allowing miracles to occur.

I felt compelled to tell my story to illustrate that there is a force trying to steer us in better directions and that it has the ability to literally save our asses at times of distress or danger. That force, whether it comes in the form of angelic or God-like intervention is ever present and exists even if you do not believe in it or know what to call it. I believe synchronicity happens to everyone, no matter what religion or faith you are – or even if you have none at all. Some experience it with more frequency.

My story unfolds showing how we attract where we are resonating. If we are resonating as victim and that is how we feel at a core level, we attract abusers. The mystery of this recounting also illustrates that your life is a series of choices. It is wise to start learning at a young age to really appreciate and love yourself. That, in itself, is an ongoing journey. Being you and comfortable in your own skin is tough and our societal structure can make it very difficult. However, by doing so, perhaps you will spare yourself some heartache along your way in life. Further, you will allow the true you to emerge and possibly transform others.

For those that are a bit older, I hope you see within these pages that no matter how screwed up someone may seem, they can turn things around and make their life better. Overall, we all grow through adversity. Mediocrity never produces anything above a safe status quo that can slip into the questions of: Why am I here? What have I done with my life? Though we may long for an easier life with no hurts or struggles to overcome, unfavorable circumstances can often serve as true catalysts for inner growth.

For people who have suffered trauma of any sort at the hands of others, I want to include a "trigger warning" in this book. If the text you are reading upsets you in a particular section, please skip to the next chapter. I also want to sadly acknowledge that so many have suffered trauma and abuse much worse than mine. Yet, trauma is not set up to be a contest of who can endure the worst. Trauma will try to own us. Even if we tame it like a large pet dragon, that animal will still sometimes rear up and breathe fire. I have learned that we have the power to subdue it.

Ultimately, my journey is exposed giving birth to a new sense of self worth and finally learning to love myself and others in a way that was not possible, except through healing. Please join me in this chronicle of being touched by divine synchronicity and entering my world of dreams.

Beyond Coincidence

"Fate is fluid ... Destiny is in the hands of men."
~ *The Man In The High Castle*

For the past several years, people all around the world are seeing consecutive numbers, especially when checking the time. Certainly, this happens to me frequently. Having not worn a watch for more than a decade, I am not one to check the time often. I do not work at a job where I have to be constantly cognizant of the time, either counting down the minutes to leave or be at a particular appointment. When this is happening with greater frequency, it is not unusual to question if it is more than coincidence.

Often, when I do check the time out of curiosity, I find it is 11:11 or some other set of identical numbers. Some believe this is a message that you are in your flow ... on the right path. Today, while having what I felt was an enlightened thought, I looked at the clock and saw 12:12. For me, this means that I am in sync with the divine God source and my higher purpose. 444 is another number which many believe means angels are nearby or watching over.

Recently, I sent a text to someone dear letting them know I was feeling extremely positive and proactive that day. I looked at the time of the text and it was 11:11.

This number phenomenon is becoming more common as we hear people talking about it all around the world. It could be due to those who are awakening to the deeper aspects of themselves that speak in symbols. Indeed, our dreams are often full of symbols and feelings that can reflect the inner workings of our emotional bodies and minds. Yet, my synchronicities and dreams have gone beyond identical numbers.

Similar seemingly simple occurrences were a lifelong study for Dr. Carl G. Jung, who defined the word "synchronicity" and brought forth the concept in the late 1920's. However, he did not complete a full opinioned thesis on synchronicity until 1952 in his work titled *Synchronicity An Acausal Connecting Principle*.

During his lifetime, Jung worked with many great minds including Albert Einstein, Wolfgang Pauli, and Sigmund Freud. What I found astounding in reading Jung's works, especially his later letters and speeches, was that he went well into his seventies still exploring synchronicity, especially in relation to the paranormal. He often utilized esoteric forms of experimentation including astrology, dreams and telepathy.

I was also quite struck by Jung's own frustration at attempting to fully define synchronicity and all the parameters associated with it. Like Jung, I had lived through so many "beyond coincidence" events. I had attempted to put meaning to these experiences, always falling short of a concise, complete discourse on it. To precisely define synchronicity seems very doable, yet once defined, it can be changing. It is not unlike the Tao or the constant potential existing in a zero point field described by our physics of late. It shows itself to be a mutable force that at times mimics fate, yet cannot be solely defined as such.

If a great mind such as Carl Jung's had struggled, then I felt better in my attempts to make sense of it all. In Jung's foreword, he writes of how difficult it was earlier in life to write a concise interpretation of synchronicity. He credits waiting later in life to do so and accumulating so many synchronicities himself as not only further proof of the phenomena, but additional evidence to base his findings.

Perhaps I have been privileged to experience so many episodes of this nature, simply because I was so bent on failing forward. Perhaps, someone beyond the physical was trying desperately to steer me in certain directions. Throughout, dreams, synchronicity and intuitive gnosis play a huge role in shaping my life events.

I suspended the judgment process a long time ago. As part of my evolutionary process, I learned to look gratefully toward each and every experience and any lesson it provided, no matter the anger or grief associated with it. Yet I also began to see that I could assist myself to experience better things through contact with my dreams, fueling my desires, and then watch the synchronicities begin to unfold. This is a gift that we all can access – a journey in making things happen.

Now, let us begin with the tale of how this force spoke to one of my grandfathers on a dark night in the countryside.

Hobos

"Listen to the wind, it talks. Listen to the silence, it speaks. Listen to your heart, it knows."
~ Native American proverb

As a young girl, I spent each weekday after school with my maternal grandparents until my mother would get off work. I also spent a good portion of summer break with them as well. I was sometimes bored, but always shielded from my mother's wrath while with my grandparents.

Retired, Grandpa and I would often play gin rummy or another card game during the winter in their small living room while watching old western movies on the portable color television. In the late 1960's and early 1970's, we did not have cable television. There were only three local channels, of which two came in well and the other was intermittent. Our choices were limited, but we were just happy it was in color instead of black and white. You don't miss what hasn't been invented yet.

Often, Grandpa would jump from his seat on the couch when the big fuzzy horizontal lines began rolling continuously up and down the screen. He would give the television a quick hit on top with his closed fist. The rolling would stop. "There!" he would say with a pleased look on his face. Grandpa returned to the couch and our card game until a few minutes later when the television would again be rolling the fuzzy lines up and down the screen and he would give it a good hit again.

Soon, my grandmother would have something yummy prepared in the kitchen for us. It was a sunny room with a combination of installed white wood cabinets on the sink wall and free standing metal cabinetry on another wall. A yellow rectangle table graced the center of the room with silver chrome metal rim and matching chairs, now a great art deco find. I'm sure they considered all their "stuff" old and outdated. It was, however, functional so they did not seem to care. They had very limited means.

My grandfather would sit at the head of the table and I would sit on the side. Always, we had to beg grandma to sit down and eat with us. It seemed she was still up preparing, overdoing, serving and not thinking enough of herself. Finally, she would sit down and we would all be together at the table.

There was a bathroom off the kitchen with two steps leading up to it. It was an add-on as the house when originally built had no lavatory. I spent much time as a toddler and young child singing "One for the money, two for the show, three to get ready and four to go", finally making my jump off the steps on the word go. I was a physically active child, often swinging my legs wildly in the kitchen while supporting my body with my arms – one on the table and one on the free standing metal cabinet which was almost the same table height. Often, I've thought about this behavior and how my grandparents never said a word to me about the intense activity. Today, I would probably be labeled as hyperactive. Looking back, I was just being active. I had energy and it needed to be expended. I loved feeling my body move whether it was through dance, sports or leg swinging like a little monkey.

Grandpa loved to show me odd things. He waited until the equinox to get an egg out of the refrigerator and try to make it stand on its end. This seemed impossible and he tried to make me understand that on this day of the year only could this be done. Now, it could just be he had the right raw eggs and a very patient magic because he would finally get one to stand upright for a certain length of time. This would excite me greatly but I had no way of capturing the moment and making it stand still in time except in my mind. I had no film camera handy.

Grandfathers can also tell grandchildren many stories, but the one that follows stuck with me for life. Grandpa seemed emotionally intense as he retold the tale. It held a lot of meaning for him and you could sense that in his voice and his brilliant blue eyes.

His story was prompted by my question, "Grandpa, do you believe in Jesus?" I was eleven or twelve years old and on fire with the Lord Jesus. I had taken it upon myself to go to church at a young age, without my parents. My father, an engineer, was very scientifically oriented and said he did not believe in God. My mother believed in God, but did not attend church at the time.

I became a member of a Southern Baptist church. A bus, owned by this organization and driven by the father of one of my school friends, would come around each Sunday picking me up and bringing me back home. At this church, I made more friends, became "saved", sang in the choir, played on the basketball and softball teams. I loved this new group of people I was becoming connected to! I wanted my family to be "saved" and not go to hell like the preacher told everyone would happen if they did not accept Jesus as their Lord and Savior.

To keep from ending up in hell, you had to make your way down to the altar at the end of a sermon. You would then make a pledge in front of the congregation that you were giving yourself to Jesus as the Son of God; that you accepted that Jesus died on the cross for you; and that you were asking to be forgiven for your sins. You would also be baptized, not normally that day, but at the next scheduled baptism ceremony. Of course, you did have to feel true remorse for your sins and unworthiness. Not to worry, the preacher had a way of bringing that out of you each Sunday.

My grandfather had been a handsome man in his younger days and you could still see that spark in his eyes that now held a quiet wisdom that spoke to you, even when he wasn't saying a thing. He loved gardening and the earth. He disliked the government and interference with people's lives. He lived very simply, yet was content. Grandpa was not an overachiever by any means. If anything, I knew my parents helped him and my grandmother over the years with certain things like home telephone service. My grandparents did not attend church. I knew they had attended church when younger, but had long stopped going.

So as I sat with Grandpa at the yellow kitchen table one afternoon and asked him if he believed in Jesus, he answered me in this way:

"When my brothers and I were young, we wanted to travel. We wanted to see things and get off the farm. We were out to experience life. One night it almost killed us. We were young hobos, jumping trains to get about. We had caught a train and jumped off before the next station into town so as not to get caught by the law. We carried our nap sacks and we were having the time of our lives going all around the country and seeing things we had never seen before.

Hiking through the countryside, we soon found ourselves in complete pitch dark. We wanted to go as far as we could before finding a place to lie down and sleep for the night. All of a sudden, something told me – it was like it urged me in a strong voice in my mind to stop right in the hell where we were and not to go further. It was not my voice I heard, but the voice of someone else. I told my brothers about the voice. My brothers laughed at me and there was some argument about walking further, but I insisted, dropping my pack on the ground. They followed suit and we stopped right there, making a place to lie down and sleep until morning.

When we awoke, I could see why I had that feeling and heard that strong voice. If we had stepped just ten more feet, we would have walked off a cliff. So, yes, I believe there is something, but I don't know what it is. It could be an angel. It could be God. It is something that I can't name to know for sure. But, I do believe it. I know there is more to everything than what we see with our eyes and hear with our ears. There is something."

In my late twenties, this same grandfather had a heart attack at home. The ambulance took him to the closest hospital and I met my other family members there as soon as I found out. My mother, uncle, aunt, and grandmother were there in the ICU waiting room. He could only receive two visitors for fifteen minutes. Time passed and my grandmother and I went to his room together.

He was very active for an intensive care patient. Sitting straight up in the bed, he stated that he wanted the hell out of there. He wanted to go home. He was uncomfortable with all the intravenous tubes and pulled at a couple of them. I spoke to him calmly telling him what I thought a doctor would want me to say, trying to reassure him that all was for his own good and that he needed to relax.

Something was very different about my grandpa. I felt or saw something that just spoke to me inside and I knew he was not going to come home. I played the game with him, however, that he would and to just try and relax. Yet, something told me that this might be the last time we talked.

Our fifteen minute visiting time limit was up and I took his hand right before leaving the room and squeezed it tight. Feeling a sense of urgency to say something significant, I said, "Grandpa, remember when you told me about you and your brothers jumping trains, being hobos and the cliff?" His eyes lit up and met mine with a deep gaze of knowing. He nodded affirmatively, very deliberately and slowly. His frantic movements and nervousness were abated. My eyes met his and I said, "Remember, there is something grandpa. There is something!"

As I took my frail grandmother back to the family waiting area after our visit, I broke down in convulsive tears as soon as the door closed and we were passing the nurse's station. I knew he was not coming home. I absolutely knew it. When I arrived where my mother, uncle and aunt were waiting, they asked me what was wrong. I told them my feeling. Grandpa will not come home. He's not going to make it. They all reassured me that I was wrong. They told me that he was one thousand percent better than when he arrived at the hospital, his skin tone blue. They went to some length telling me the good prognosis from the doctor and trying to calm me down. They all really believed that grandpa was going to be here longer and come home. I said, "No, there is something I felt. He is not coming home."

A few days later, my grandpa was still at the hospital and had actually been transferred out of intensive care. He was in a regular room and doing very well. I went to see him and this time we were alone. Now, I felt I was wrong. Evidently, my initial feeling was unjustified. Perhaps, I was just overly emotional. My mom and uncle must be right. He was going to make it home very soon. Because I believed this, I never said the things I later felt I should have said. It was the last time I saw him. He did not come home from the hospital. He passed on into the next realm and his absence hit me hard.

When we received the call that he was gone, I asked everyone, "How? What happened?" He was out of ICU, going to be fine according to the doctor. All they could say is that "sometimes people get better for the worse". What that means is that you are bad off physically, you get better temporarily, and then boom, you're gone.

My grandfather was not ready to commit to an entire religion or attending church. He made his assessment of God based upon his experiences in life. I am sure his intuition spoke to him all the time.

Yet, he made it clear that this was beyond that voice within. It was a voice outside of him that urged him and his brothers to stop right away and not go further into the dark.

Some say when people are ready to pass on, their aura starts fading, slipping into the next realm. Perhaps, that is what I was sensing. I cannot put into words what I perceived, but it was there nonetheless. Grandpa was lively, very animated, sitting upright in the ICU, wanting those damn tubes out of his body. He did not look like a man that was leaving us, but he was and in some way, I knew this.

My mother stayed with my grandmother the first night after his death and actually slept with her. She stated they saw green lights flicker through the room very swiftly and she felt certain it was from Grandpa who was letting them know that he still existed on some level.

Often, we experience happenings that call out to the enigma we long to put a linguistic term to. This is the dilemma that Dr. Carl Jung found himself in when he defined the term synchronicity. While synchronicity does not encompass all that lies beyond human perception, its existence opens up a large hole in the unseen fabric of our experience that deserves to be fully explored.

We can feel tempted to discount synchronicity, calling it just a coincidence. If synchronicity does not fit our reality perception of how the world works, it is easy to toss it aside and call it a rare set of occurrences that are simply coincidental. Events that have a supernatural element are also discarded by some, but this is changing as science and, more specifically, physics opens up new avenues of how things operate in our universe.

Through unknown means, grandpa knew as a young hobo to stop right where he and his brothers were for the night, feeling danger imminent. I knew with a strange certainty that Grandpa would not come back home. My mother and grandmother experienced something supernatural, as a sign that life goes on.

Grandpa's story about almost walking off the cliff was told to me to cover the fact that he had a belief in something greater, but did not resonate with going to church for some reason. He was also telling me to look for this myself and to listen to the cues life might afford to me. I'm sure Grandpa had already noticed that I was a highly sensitive child.

Beginning

"Man is in the process of changing, to forms that are not of this world; grows he in time to the formless, a plane on the cycle above. Know ye, ye must become formless before ye are one with the light." –

adapted from *The Emerald Tablets of Thoth*

I have always experienced paranormal things. My first memory is being in my baby bed, not yet able to speak in words. The hallway of the small apartment my parents lived in was part of my paternal grandparents' home which had been divided, much like a duplex, to include a small section for my young parents to make a home together. The cramped square hallway, which was where my baby bed was located, had three doors. One led to the bathroom, another to my parents' bedroom, and the third to a small kitchen. The remaining wall of this square is where my bed was situated.

Inside this dark hallway of a room, I sat upright in my bed one night watching a figure of bright white light. It came close to my bed and I felt very afraid. I began to cry but it was as if I was stifled to get the noise out and I stopped suddenly. The light being had some silent control over me in a soothing, calming way. There was a communication, but I don't know what it consisted of. Resembling a bright hologram, I could make out the image of a human-like face. But it was not human, more resembling stiff bright white smoke formed together. It was as if it was made of light particles.

I know people say you cannot remember things prior to the age of three. I don't know exactly what age I was, but it would definitely be less than that. I could not talk yet and I am told I was speaking in words fluently at two. In addition, I was in a baby bed with rails. This is my first and only memory I have at my conscious recall of something beyond our ordinary human experience and it has stuck with me my entire life. It left me often questioning what it was all about and trying to understand its meaning. This is one of two conscious memories I have as an infant and both situations were highly charged with emotion.

My mother was beautiful with long legs and a friendly smile when she befriended her paperboy at only fifteen. Almost six years her senior, he convinced her parents to allow her to date. Soon thereafter, at mom's tender age of sixteen, I was born. We lived with my paternal grandparents for the first three years of my life and I remained an only child until my first sister was born when I was thirteen.

I cannot recall at what age my mother began being abusive, but it may have been occasionally right from the start. My nose is crooked and when I asked why one nostril was smaller than the other she told me it was because I had hit the dashboard, breaking my nose when my car seat did not work correctly. She was delivering newspapers on my father's route while he worked another job and attended college full time.

I have seen the car seats used during that era and if it propelled me toward the dashboard, it would have ended up falling into the floor of the car. I always wondered if she actually smacked or hit me in the face as an infant who was probably crying. With how she treated me growing up, such a scenario would not be surprising to me. This is a feeling I have that the entire truth was not told, but I have no proof. Therefore, it is not really fair to accuse her of anything regarding this.

The three of us living with my father's parents and siblings, all under one giant house gave her, as a young mother, needed help as they assisted in taking care of me. I was adored and played with frequently by my two teenage aunts. My grandparents would take turns rocking me or getting me to sleep.

We moved into a townhouse apartment when I was around three years old. I remember watching cartoons on our small black and white television many days. I also remember trying to make my mom feel better and stop crying as she sat close in front of that small television, telling me that someone had shot the President.

My mother saw me as one of two things on any given day. I was either her golden child or I was her burden and embarrassment. Due to her own feelings of low self worth, how I conducted myself was like looking at her own reflection. Her identity was very much tied with me and how I acted.

She was proud of me when I did cute things or performed in my yearly dance recital. She was equally disgusted with me when she had to take me to the doctor. I was deathly afraid of needles and it seemed to have nothing to do with pain. It had more to do with the sight of a needle piercing the skin. As I became older, I learned that if I thought about something else with great concentration, turned my head away and did not see the piercing, I could avoid passing out. Prior to that, I would faint landing on the floor each time I saw the syringe with its needle poking out the end.

My mother had little patience for me when I was ill and that was frequently. I suffered from sore throats in a chronic way and at the doctor's suggestion had my tonsils removed at about age four or five.

Still experiencing sore throats from time to time, my mother once forced Vick's Vapor Rub down my throat pushing her fingers in as far as she could as I lay in the bed. This was a horrendous experience. Later I told her (when I could speak again) that people were not supposed to eat the rub, she smacked me in the face demanding that I not tell her what to do or argue with her.

It has been noted by many great metaphysical thinkers, including Louise Hay, that children often suffer sore throats because they feel they cannot speak their minds to the adults around them. Unable to give a voice to their thoughts, dis-ease can manifest in the body.

At a young age, I began to see people in my room at night. They did not appear like the luminescent light being. They looked like real people. The old woman was the scariest to me and the one that I would see the most. Lying in my bed and feeling the hairs stand up on my arms. I would glance over toward the closed louvered closet door and there she was – just standing in front of the door looking at me. She never said anything and she looked as real as anyone would look in the dark. At times, she would change her facial expression from what seemed to be inquisitive to a deep scowling.

I frequently held my breath and stayed as still as possible thinking she would perhaps not notice me. It was not uncommon for me to slowly inch the blanket over my face, hoping she would not know I was there. Yet, she was staring straight at me. On these nights I often would lie stone still, barely breathing until I would get up the nerve to run into my parents room. I would sleep on the floor beside their bed until morning. It would take a lot of self-talk to be brave enough to make the sudden move out of my bed and out the door to their room.

Another anomaly was that many nights, as I would try to fall asleep, there was a noise and visual pattern going on in my brain that would prevent me from doing so. I will try to describe it. As I would lie there with closed eyes, I would experience two different tones. One tone was a low vibration humming type noise and the other tone was a higher pitch. They would alternate, never both at the same time. Accompanying this noise would be a visual pattern I was seeing with my eyelids closed. They were two distinctly different visual images that were moving in a consistent pattern with the sound.

In other words, if I heard the high pitch sound, I saw one visual pattern and the lower sound had its own visual pattern. There was symmetry to them consisting of lines intersecting. One was a tighter pattern that the other. This would often go on for some time before I would finally fall asleep. I remember complaining to my parents about these patterns and noise tones but I don't think they knew what to think about it.

I also experienced sleepwalking and bedwetting. Sometimes, I would find myself in the bathtub with my pajamas on. I would wake up wondering how I got there and how long I had been in the water. I remember my parents finding me walking around the house a few times while asleep. Again, they would shake me or talk to me until I realized what was going on. Yet, I never fully understood what had happened. I would just finally wake up, finding myself somewhere other than my bed.

The last sleepwalking episode I had was as late as sixteen years old wherein I found myself in my pajamas several houses down the street waiting for the school bus and afraid I was late because no other students were there waiting with me. Eventually, I awoke and realized I must have come to the bus stop in my sleep. I did not remember walking out the door, much less leaving my bed.

As a small child, my core personality was soft hearted and empathetic. Once, I rode in the back seat of the car to the dentist office with my family. We were stopped at a traffic light and there was a man lying on the sidewalk. I asked why. My father said he was a "bum" and that he was homeless. The fact that I had always had a home and a large extended family around me made it hard to comprehend that someone would have to sleep on the sidewalk, having no home. Tears streamed down my cheeks just thinking of this man's situation.

Mom worked outside the home during this early life phase. Luckily, grandparents and aunts could be counted on to care for me. By the time I was school age, my mother was very harsh with me most mornings. I dreaded the last step of hair brushing before I would head out of the house to walk to the bus stop. I was told each day that my hair was "nothing but rats". My mother would say this in a very angry tone and brush my hair so hard I would cry. The more I cried, the harder she brushed. Sometimes she would smack me in the face as well, especially if I turned my head the wrong way to avoid further pain. At times she would also hit me with the backside of the brush.

There were many mornings I headed to the bus stop drying tears on my red cheeks, trying to look normal to the other children who would be there waiting. Inside, I felt there was something so unlovable about me. My mom had to be right. She knew and I didn't. I was defective in so many ways. Rats in my hair, peeing in my bed. What in the hell was wrong with me? I learned to try and take as much of her pain during the hair brushing as I could stand without crying. If she saw me cry, her fury would be worse. She would actually say, "Now if you cry, it's really going to hurt."

My mother was conditioning me without even knowing she was doing it. Be the shiny good girl and make me look like a great mother and you may get praise. Be my embarrassment or a hassle for me and you will receive at the very least my thoughts about how inadequate you are and at the most, a beating.

My mother was susceptible to large fits of rage. I never knew when it would occur or what may cause it. In addition to smacking me around, she said a lot of very hurtful things. There was shoving, kicking, and sometimes choking. Other than a few bruises or red marks on my face that would fade fairly soon, I did not show physical signs of abuse. Bruises could have come about from falling or playing too hard outside. I am thankful I never endured broken bones or severe injury as some children do. Yet, it truly was the words she screamed during these attacks that cut me the most.

My father would later blame it on hormones, but it persisted like a well worn grooved habit of her being unhappy or stressed about her circumstances and striking out at me in her frustration. I say 'later' because for years my father did not know the extent of what went on in our house and if I tried to tell him what mother had done to me, she would call me a liar and say I was an overly sensitive, dramatic child. Sometimes she would deny anything at all had happened. Other times, she would convince my father that I was grossly exaggerating what had occurred.

I was an only child until age thirteen when my first sister was born. I did have one close aunt that I would complain to about the abuse from my mother. Now, you have to realize that as a child, I didn't know about the word "abuse". In the 1960's, it was not a mainstream term and even if it were, children may not understand its language use. What I did know was that there was something wrong with my mother and that it was not normal the way she was talking to me and treating me in private. I would reveal some of this to my aunt and she always seemed to empathize, but tell me that I should make sure not to upset her so I could avoid it. Unfortunately, that was not possible.

It took many years to realize that my mother always had to have someone to beat up on verbally and physically. When my sisters and I had all left the nest many years later, she started in on my dad and this remains so to this day. While age has slowed her somewhat, it still happens with too much regularity. My father, approaching eighty years old, stated recently that she was on the verge of being physically violent with him just a couple of years ago. The verbal abuse is a consistent thing he endures.

She will belittle our father in front of us (her children). According to her, he is the cause of all her problems. Yet my father provided very well for her financially and has never been abusive to her. My father exhibits codependent behavior. The fact that he did not step in and stop the abuse puts him at fault as well. He has never set clear boundaries with her.

But my mother turns on and off like a faucet. In fact, much of the extended family will say that she runs hot or cold. It has been my lay opinion as I grew older that she suffered from personality disorders. She has control over when she will turn into this monster of a woman. And the realization of this made me furious at times because I could not say to myself that she could not help her behavior. She could.

Yet, if you told any of her friends this was going on, they would not -- absolutely could not believe it. In public, she was someone else entirely. I was always astounded at how my mother could beat the crap out of me and then speak with a friend or relative in person or on the phone shortly thereafter with a cheerful tone and completely different personality than the one she just displayed. I would be huddled in a corner, possible rocking myself back and forth in a fetal position and crying. My mother would be laughing and cutting up with the person on the telephone as if nothing had happened.

I learned to walk on eggshells at home which is not an admirable trait. It is something you do to try and survive. I learned to try and do things to please my parents as much as I could. Anything I did that was not pleasing to her was seen as a personal attack and she came at me with all of her craziness. "I hate you!" rolled off her tongue. "I wish you were never born. You are nothing but a burden to me." These were frequent phrases of my mother when she was angry and just about any little thing could set this off. Perhaps I had not cleaned my room, pushing stuff under my bed instead of putting it away. She was also often angry about the bedwetting saying I was just too lazy to get up and go to the bathroom. I was slapped in the face frequently for hardly anything. Shoving and pushing me around was another frequent maneuver.

Secretly, I wished for a big brother who would right these wrongs and set dad straight on what mom was doing. I needed someone to save me, but there was no one and I was not to be believed when I tried to ask for help. No one understood the extent of what my mother was doing to me. With her ability to control her rage enough not to leave lasting marks, who would not know that I was lying or exaggerating? I feared her and sometimes when she would just raise her arm enthusiastically to make a point with someone in a conversation I would flinch automatically, involuntarily bringing my hand up to cover my face. During her beatings, I had also learned how to curl into a ball, cover my face with my hands while she batted away at me.

The same day these episodes happened, my mother would almost always come into my room that night to tuck me in. She would stroke my forehead and the top of my head and tell me how sorry she was, often between real tears that she would shed. She would tell me she really did not mean it and seemed very sincere. I remember feeling stiff initially when she would do this. A part of me deeply wanted to believe her and my heart would eventually melt.

Forgiveness came easily from me because inside I believed I was causing a good deal of this. There was something so horrible about me that I was making mommy act this way. Each time I forgave her, I closed down a little portion of myself each time – the part of me that really knew what was true. And the abuse was happening with such frequency that I knew it would probably continue. I desperately wanted to believe her when she would tell me, "I'm sorry. This will never happen again."

When the next trauma occurred at her hands, I felt so betrayed for trusting and forgiving her. To me, this meant she really was not sorry because she kept doing it. I had started out as an amateur stuffing my feelings deep into an unknown place. I was quickly becoming an expert at not feeling. This was the only way I could cope with a mother who had these fits of anger and my own increasing feelings of unworthiness.

Frequently, she would take me shopping the next day, as if something material would make up for the hurt she had inflicted. It seemed it was all she knew to do and she was trying to erase what had happened. It also could have been a way to get me to side with her, not tell anyone and bribe me. But I did tell at times and no one did anything.

My mother had grown up very poor, not having an indoor bath until just before puberty. She did not finish high school and often felt not good enough compared to other students. Her childhood clothing was not as nice and she would never experience things at a young age like playing the piano or tennis. Buying me material things after the abuse probably seemed like love to her.

I believe my mother did love me in the best way she could. She was overwhelmed with her own emotions and physiological problems. With my father gone quite a bit, she was alone and probably often felt unloved or underappreciated. I was not a difficult child to handle. In fact, I tried to please my parents all the time. Behavior challenges did not present themselves until later in my teen years. I both feared and loved my mother. I wanted her approval. Due to the cruel and sudden outbursts, I didn't trust her. It would shape my relationships with women a good part of my life. Women were wonderful creatures, but could they be trusted not to suddenly turn on you?

One particular day, I had been playing with a new friend I had made up the street, an adopted girl from Korea. She was lovely with her almond shaped eyes and another friend of mine was along as well. I lost track of time. I was supposed to be home at a certain hour. When I arrived late, my mother was furious. She had been vacuuming the long hallway that led to the bedrooms off the family room area. She took the canister style vacuum cleaner attachments and started hitting me with them, yelling how she hated me again – stating how she wished I was never born. I thought she might kill me. I cried and begged her to stop. That did not seem to help. The violence just intensified.

On this day, my father came in shortly after the vacuum cleaner incident. I was still on the hallway floor crying hysterically, hyperventilating between breaths. I tried telling my dad what my mom had done. It was hard to slow my breath to get the words out in a cohesive manner. I begged my father, reaching out, grabbing his pant leg asking him to please, please divorce her. My mother mocked me and told my father I was such an overly dramatic child. She told him I was crazy. The scene was so fresh, I had the slight impression that my father did question what was going on. As far as I know, he didn't follow up on it.

In today's world, you could put electronic devices in your home to record what went on when you were not there. Oh, how I wish people had known the extent of the occurrences that were happening to me, a defenseless child.

My physical abuse stopped when I became large and strong enough to stop my mother. Again, in the hallway where the vacuum cleaner incident had occurred, she went after me one day. Slapping, hitting me with her fist on my arms, I suddenly felt courageous and grabbed her hard by the shoulders and threw her up against the closet door. I held her there with all my might. Looking straight into her eyes because we were now almost the same height I said, "You will never hit me again, do you hear me? You will never touch me again." She was startled and she felt how much muscle and power I had as I pinned her on the closet door. I let her go and walked away. She said nothing. I had set my first boundary with her.

So disturbed with my relationship with my mother, I learned to stuff my feelings deep inside in an invisible place where I could not feel them directly. I would not give her the satisfaction of knowing she was upsetting me any longer. I ignored her when she let her vicious mouth loose on me. That verbal abuse continued for a long time – as in decades. Stuffing our emotions is a short term solution and it only hurts us in the long run. Over the years, these emotions would rise up and rear their ugly heads in numerous ways.

I picked up the idea that I was faulty and a bad child. I felt like I did not deserve. I had received so many material items from my extended family and my parents. This point was often driven home to me by my mother in her anger. I was receiving mixed messages. All of my family loved me and did great things for me – gifted me materially – including my mother. Yet the emotional tantrums and harsh words made me feel like nothing. At a deep level, I vacillated between two extremes: I either felt confident and that I could achieve so much or I felt I really didn't deserve to breathe.

Why is it that the negative things hold more impact for us? Is it because they are so emotionally charged? In my adult life, this set up a pattern. Propelled by the side of me that said I could achieve things, I would work hard to do so and would manifest wonderful situations for myself. But it was always a struggle to keep it. I continued playing the program in my subconscious that I did not really deserve it and this showed itself in so many ways that impacted not just myself, but everyone connected with me.

My confusion about relationships and what healthy good love really looked like was warped and I made poor decisions. I was on a search for approval, adoration and love.

Forgiveness is something that has come in layers over time. I felt that something was wrong with her brain. It always bothered me that she could control herself enough not to act out like this when anyone else was present. With my propensity to be nice, I fooled myself at times into thinking I had fully forgiven her. Certainly, I have been encouraged by religious dogma and more esoteric spiritual teachings to forgive her. So, I would process parts of it and believe that I had forgiven her.

    I would then find that situations would happen and I would realize I had not completely processed this and given full forgiveness. Right now I am in a peaceful state with her, but I know that could change. So, I am careful about not having too much contact, but enough to maintain the relationship letting her know I care.

    Unfortunately, I may never experience a deep relationship with my mother. You just cannot accomplish that when you don't know when she will strike verbally at you again. Once the damage is done, you may forgive this act or that, but you cannot completely forget about it. Completely forgetting is even harder than forgiving.

    So, I want you to know that I have forgiven certain aspects of this situation. This is honest and I am not perfect. I am working toward a better solution as I find it and I do feel I am getting very close.

    If you love someone, you need to be able to trust them. You need to know that they will not turn on you. Relationships with people are like trees. It takes a long time for a tree to grow. It only takes a few minutes to take it down with a chainsaw. Much as you want to live and be happy, you try to shrug it off, stuffing your feelings deep inside of you for no one to see.

    If my mother were a boyfriend I had encountered, I could break up and be rid of her for the rest of my life. She's my mother though. As an adult woman, I have broken up with her before, not speaking to her for months. At other times, my mother has stepped up and been like a loving best friend.

    I include this information for you, as the reader, to have a base understanding. I am not one who has gone through my life blaming everything on mommy. But I want you to know the dynamics and it is also an injustice to withhold and not tell my story. When we cover up for people and make excuses for them, we stay in victim roles and cannot progress toward our greater good and the purposes we came here to fulfill.

    Certainly, many other people have endured worse from their own families or strangers. "Life is hard." you hear people say. "Pull yourself up by your bootstraps and go on." Well… that's just what I did, but not always very gracefully. The same lessons would go round and round on the wheel of my life for years before fully comprehending what I was doing to myself.

Leaving The Church

"Religion is belief in someone else's experience. Spirituality is having your own experience." – Deepak Chopra

The Southern Baptist church I attended without my parents had a huge congregation. There are "mega churches" now. For that time, our church membership and attendance was large, making it difficult for people to find a parking place on Sunday morning. I rode with friends or caught the church's bus that came around our neighborhood. I also rode my bicycle quite a bit. My mother would hardly drive me anywhere. She wanted nothing to do with picking me up from cheerleading or other sports I participated in. She always said she "just couldn't". My father would help with this, but he was working two demanding jobs and rarely home.

A separate building at the church had been built for playing basketball and other indoor activities. Many of our youth classes were in this same building. There was a boy that I really liked who played piano at the church. I wanted to say that we were girlfriend and boyfriend and I suppose we were, but he seemed quite non-committal with me. It wasn't that he seemed interested in another girl. He was driven by his pursuits of music and not much into the whole courtship thing.

Nevertheless, we would hold hands and look like a couple. I sang in the choir as well as solo. He accompanied me and a traveling evangelist to smaller churches in the country on some Sundays in the summer. He would play piano and I would sing religious songs that we loved. These churches were so small and intimate. Often, the three of us would be invited back to the pastor's home after the service to eat dinner with their entire family. The weather was beautiful on these days and life was as well. I look back on these innocent memories with great fondness.

I also made a friend named Cary who was very steeped in the evangelical side of Christianity. Religion and bible talk seeped out of her every pore. She was a couple of years older, as I was twelve or thirteen at the time. Cary sang extremely well and I wanted her to help me with my singing. She had a huge, powerful alto voice and she was quite the instrument.

Cary was obsessed with demon possession and avoiding it. Once, she spent the night with me and stayed up for hours talking about demons and how they can possess people, what power they have and how Jesus can keep them away. She would say repeatedly, "All you have to do is say: In the blood of Jesus Christ, I command you to leave."

I couldn't sleep that night. She had me scared out of my wits. I finally stopped hanging around her because she was so full of the demon talk and it made me feel like they would creep up on me at anytime and try to take me over. Later in life, I learned that we attract what we focus on the most. Trying to go to sleep at night with this fear that would overcome me was not something I felt good about, so our friendship had to end.

There was something inside me that hungered for spiritual attunement. This is why I had made a way to go to church without my parents. Plus, it gave me more time away from home and that was a place where good or bad things could happen with my mother.

My feelings about the church itself were mixed. I wanted to focus on singing and the love of Jesus. I did not like all the talk about the tribulation and I always felt that God could not be as cruel as he was described in the Old Testament. This God they spoke of struck entire cities down, turned people into pillars of salt, asked you to sacrifice your children. This always felt incongruent with the message of Christ.

Our church also purchased real estate for a retreat area about an hour away in distance. Basically, it was a farm that had access to the river at a certain point. They intended to make it into a Christian retreat for all the church members. It was in its first rough stages when I went there.

The property had a barn and a gender contest ensued between who was going to sleep in the farmhouse and who would be in the second story of the huge barn. The boys won the farmhouse, putting us girls out in the barn. Huge in size, the barn upstairs could sleep forty or fifty girls. We all had those small cots you find in so many camping situations and as lights went out, things started flying through the air. I hunkered into my sleeping bag on the cot, completely covering my head, while everyone screamed at the bats. Our teenage adrenal glands were in overdrive with these small flying, freaky mammals. We all ended up turning on the lights to try and sleep, thinking that the bats would prefer only the dark. The bloodcurdling screams continued with everyone eventually running to the farmhouse and sending the boys to the barn.

After prayer in the morning and breakfast, we headed out into the warm summer day. We walked down a trail that led to the river. There was a shallow area where you could wade in up to five feet for those that were not swimmers. Additionally, there were huge cliffs you could hike up to where the more adventurous of the campers would jump into the water below. I first made my way up to the cliffs. You could run and jump into the water below or you could swing out on a rope. Timing was everything with the rope. The fear element of dropping into the water and letting go of the rope was exhilarating. You had to let go at the right time. This meant you needed to swing very far out before you let go and dropped into the water. It was a lot of fun and I found myself and my friends doing this over and over again.

After a couple of hours of dropping from the cliff into the river and then hiking back up to the area repeatedly, I started running out of energy. I decided to stay in the shallow area and just be in the water with my friends for awhile. Our youth pastor was there with us as a chaperone and leader of the youth group. There were other adult volunteer chaperones in the cliff area with the teens.

Suddenly, our youth pastor swam up to me, quickly poking his head out of the water, his dark straight hair dripping with water and grabbed one of my breasts while his arm was still underwater. I wanted to think it was accidental, like someone inadvertently brushing against you. Yet, it was a hard squeeze. His expression showed it was deliberate as his eyes looked right into mine and he smiled while he did it. I pushed his arm away and stomped off into shore. Shocked, I could not believe he did that.

Shortly thereafter, we all picked up our gear and headed back to the farmhouse area. As I walked up the trail with one of my girlfriends, I told her what happened. She laughed and rebuffed me as if the youth pastor could not have done such a thing. She said he must have bumped me by accident. I decided to keep the subject quiet and not talk about it if I was not to be believed by one of my best friends.

The worst part of it all was that he was the son of our Pastor. He was also the brother of my dear friend's boyfriend. He was married and knew better. This was something I would have expected from one of the young twelve or thirteen year old boys, not the preacher's son and our youth pastor who also taught about God.

I wondered why he thought he could get away with that and with me. If he was looking to feel breasts, one of my friends had a huge set. The whole thing made me feel cheap, violated and stifled because I could not talk to anyone about it. If I told my parents, they would never let me go anywhere again with my friends at church. So I kept it quiet.

Everything we do to each other has impact – for good or bad. He was like a snake in the grass to me, waiting to strike when he thought I wasn't looking. I hated him and I began to look at all the words that spewed from his mouth and his father's in a much different light. It was the unraveling of religion for me. Sure, he only grabbed me, but it was the look. It was the violating circumstances. He knew I was powerless to do anything and that is what rapists do. They try to take away other people's power.

I was very sports oriented and played on just about every team you can imagine at church and school. I downgraded my activity at church and focused more on school sports. I ran track, played tennis, learned gymnastics and eventually tried out for the junior varsity cheerleading squad. Our school had an extremely competitive cheerleading program that had won national awards. To be chosen, you had to look good, be well-liked or popular, plus have considerable physical endurance and gymnastic skills. The final decision of whether or not you would be on the squad was made by the entire student body as they filled the bleachers in the large indoor assembly hall. I made the squad, but just barely being one of the two alternates. I think this played in nicely with my intent to receive the position and my pervasive feelings of not being good enough.

I loved cheerleading and all the girls on our squad. We had many days together practicing and pushing physical and mental boundaries. We had great bonding times at cheerleading camp at the University of Kentucky. Arising to begin work out and practice early, we'd end the night being crazy girls playing tricks on each other such as putting sardines in someone's bed.

At home, I found myself looking at my father's books. He had a couple of books on astrology that drew my interest, along with a book of Plato's writings and a few books on UFO's. Becoming immersed in the study of astrology and Plato, religion fell away for me at this time. I had read the bible now two times from front to back in church. The red lettered words of Jesus in the New Testament made sense to me, but many other things did not. I definitely had a problem with the vengeful God described in many parts of the Old Testament.

I allowed my interests to follow where they went. Sometimes the subjects I studied felt too heavy for me. I would mentally set those aside and focus only on what resonated with me at the time. I have always studied this way. It has been refreshing to later pick up things I avoided before out of indoctrinated fear, disinterest, or the lack of ability to comprehend at the time.

I came to look at what the youth minister did as a gift. His action set into motion a deep questioning. Perplexed by many of the church teachings and witness to much hypocrisy, I began to analyze things with a new light shown on the entire situation. There were really good people at the church who seemed to live what they believed. However, they were few in number. I realized that churches were made up of people and we are all here to learn, grow and correct things within ourselves.

Within most Christian churches, you are taught not to question anything when it comes to the Bible and their interpretation of it. The idea that it could have been manipulated or there are some inaccuracies is heresy. Yet, I did question things because there seemed to be so many incongruent things I came across.

I grew to see Christianity as something that was created quite a few years after Jesus had been physically martyred. I found myself still loving Jesus and believing that his metaphorically veiled teachings were the right way to live and be. Yet, now I felt I had no religion and was starting over. I had been "saved" and now everyone around me that used that term would say I was lost or backslidden. I was definitely lost, but it was not anything anyone could save me from, except myself and a hidden force that would begin to appear in my life at times when I needed it most.

Religion did not leave me entirely. The doctrine of hell, judgment, and demon possession were more deeply ingrained than I knew. It would take years for me to lose the fear portions of religion. It would take time to see how Jesus really fit into the picture of the spirituality of mankind that made sense to me.

I fell away from the church for good and right into the arms of danger.

The Con Man

"Never trust people who promise to make you rich in a day.
They are generally crazy swindlers."

"A conscience is that still small voice that people won't listen to."

~ Carlo Collodi, *Pinocchio*

The culture I grew up in of the 1960's and 1970's revolved around the women's liberation movement, civil rights and freedoms. There were questions surrounding the assassination of John F. Kennedy, the Vietnam War, and we witnessed the counterculture movement of the hippies. Prominent movie stars included Raquel Welch, Ann Margaret, Bridget Bardot and Marilyn Monroe, even though she had long passed. We had just put a human on the moon.

One of my favorite things to play as a child was movie stars. My best friend and I would dress up and pretend like we were stars going to special parties and events. I had attended dance school since a young age. I loved creating singing and dancing shows in our formal living room which was devoid of furniture and open to the dining room. My parents would have friends over for dinner and I would organize the children present to participate in a "show" where we all would play different parts. We would use construction lighting belonging to my father as our stage spotlight.

In my heart, I wanted to be someone famous. Being so sports oriented much of my life, I loved dance and singing as well. I wanted to feel the adoration of others and be a part of something huge. I knew if you wanted something like this, you would need to head for Hollywood.

I was looking for others to validate me and give me a love I could not offer myself – a love that had been robbed by the constant messages of being such a burden to my mother.

After leaving the church as a teen, I secured my first summer part-time job at McDonald's. I was often put on dining room clean up. There was a man who would come to the restaurant daily. Over time, he befriended me. He was actually a con artist and pimp, but I didn't know that or even what those terms meant at the time.

He went by the name Smitty and he seemed to know the right questions to ask me. Not attractive at all, he was short, stout and somewhat muscular build with strawberry blonde hair and a ruddy pock marked complexion. Over many visits and time, Smitty gained my trust as he would continue to ask me questions, listen intently and appear to empathize with my problems at home.

One thing I remember about his demeanor was that he stared at me constantly. Oh my, he had this transfixed gaze that stayed on me as I shuffled around the dining room wiping down tables and chairs, sweeping and cleaning up. It bothered me and I would walk by him and say, "Stop staring at me." He would always smile and say something apologetic.

As an older, wiser woman, I know this stare. It is the fixed glazed look of a psychopath. They watch you the same way a cat will study a mouse and decide when to pounce. Even more, they are locking into your invisible field of energy, trying to know what you are thinking and what you are all about. Watching the movements of their prey and studying their mannerisms, looking for any and all weaknesses.

Smitty manipulated me and over time gained my trust. He gave me a ride home a couple of times after work when it was inconvenient for my mother to do so. I remember riding in the passenger seat and he was singing along with the radio in an animated way trying to be funny. Looking back, this creepy character now knew where I lived.

I never knew Smitty's age but if I were to guess I would say between twenty-five and thirty. He was old enough to know how to work me psychologically based upon what he had learned about my life and ambitions.

I remember telling him I really wanted to be a movie star or singer and that I wanted to drive a white Jaguar. Smitty would nod, encouraging me with his words and gestures. He began calling me Star as a nickname. I remember telling him I wanted to move to California because nothing was going to happen for me here.

Through his questioning on various daily visits, he knew I was unhappy at home and had problems getting along with my mother.

Smitty told me about a trip he would be making with another girl and guy out to California and if I wanted to come along with them to make my dream come true, now was the time.

I made no commitment right away and looking back, I wished I had consulted my intuition and said no way. Yet, I felt cut off from that inner knowing part of me. I had spent so much time stuffing and ignoring my feelings. When you do that, your intuitive self slips into the background. Instead, Smitty's ideas stewed in my mind and he would keep coming to the restaurant, baiting me with bits and pieces of how it could all work so perfectly.

At some point, I agreed. I remember packing more record albums in my suitcase than anything else. I had chosen mostly summer clothing and shoes. With my bag packed, I reluctantly kissed my sleeping baby sister good-bye and climbed out my bedroom window late at night to meet him at his waiting car. My sister was the only thing I felt I would miss.

As Smitty turned from secret confident to monster, any bit of innocence I had was lost after that. Instead of taking me to California, I was taken over the line into the next neighboring state less than two hundred miles from my home. I was raped repeatedly and twice at gunpoint. I was hit in the face a couple of times for not "obeying". The rebellious side of me had made itself known and even the wrong look or expression could make him violent toward me.

There was a lady and another man with us. She was older, not a young girl going to California with me as I expected. I assumed from what little I learned of her that she had been a stripper her entire adult life. I knew little to nothing about the other man. He was quiet with wire rim glasses and a thin build. He was quiet in a way that held secrets. He didn't want anyone to really know him and he seemed to lack any distinct personality traits.

The woman was probably in her late twenties but looked older. She seemed entrenched in her own addiction of pills and alcohol. She told me she was in "the life", a euphemism for living as a prostitute with a pimp. I kept thinking about this and how to get away so that I did not end up dead or in "the life".

Within the first week, I was made to work in a strip bar. This first gentlemen's club was one large dark room with a bar on one side and numerous tables and chairs throughout. On the opposite dark paneled wall of the bar was an elevated stage which contained more lighting than the entire place. A juke box sat near a room where the ladies working could change clothing or use bathroom facilities.

At the start, I was told I could dance in a bathing suit they provided. The pressure that I felt to do this was enormous. A lover of formal dance styles and a former junior varsity cheerleader, I could do this, but I had no idea of what sensual dance consisted of and I did not want to do it. This was not the limelight I had imagined.

Smitty knew how hesitant and shy I was. He understood how to work me psychologically and finally relented for me to dance with a dress on which I would eventually shed. I would then dance in the bikini. He gave me some change and told me I could pick out the music. As I perused the juke box, I chose songs that were not typical for this activity. As Gregg Allman sang *Midnight Rider*, I slowly danced in my dress on the lighted stage and for a few moments, I could blur the people in the audience out.

I was given alcohol mostly in the form of vodka mixed with orange juice. Often, Smitty would give me a black beauty or speed and he told me it was to keep me from being hungry. I do not remember if tranquilizing type pills were involved or not. My memory is fuzzy about some happenings and details, but it is very likely they could have been involved during the time I was gone. I am almost certain they were. Luckily, no one ever shot me up with heroin.

I was told a couple of times that I did not choose the right music for dancing and I totally got that. But I chose what I liked and later in life, when I heard these same songs play on the radio or anywhere, they triggered something inside me and I would think about going to work at strip bars and on a couple of occasions, did just that.

Now, I know that sounds really crazy and it is. Something you wanted to avoid and get away from and then later, you return to. I cannot explain it except to say that it was like a trauma trigger and I would actually begin to think that this is the only way I could make money I needed, despite the fact that I had other jobs and higher skills.

I would get into a financial bind because I was also horrible at managing money and find myself gravitating at night to a local strip club. As soon as I walked in, the air felt thick with the aroma of spilled drinks and mildewed carpet. I would work for a few nights dancing, make some money and then never show up again. I did this off and on and it was unpredictable when I would engage in this behavior, but it added a fresh stinky coat of paint on the cemented shame I carried around constantly, but hid from others.

Smitty was always hovering around the bar and I felt intimidated to try and tell any patrons or staff that I was in trouble and needed help. His lady companion also shadowed me when I went to the bathroom or dressing room. She was just as much part of this runaway turned kidnapping as Smitty and the other guy. Guarded – I was watched constantly.

Pressured by the bar owner, Smitty, and even the other patrons who would yell or say something when I did not take my top off, I now had to hear the same from the other dancers. They kept asking me questions that were intended to apply more pressure such as "What makes you think you're so special that you don't have to take your top off?" There were a couple of instances where I felt one or two of the girls might get violent with me. Finally, I did go topless at some point feeling so much embarrassment. I know I was making some kind of money by dancing but was not allowed to have it. It was collected by Smitty.

I felt the stares of the patrons and simultaneously felt disgust and sorrow for them. Sorrow that they were so vulnerable to female beauty and powerless in its presence, giving up their money and morality to watch, perhaps to touch or be close to it. Disgust that they were nothing more than biological robots with endless thoughts traveling through their compromised alcohol brains while they gawked, panted and tried to keep their tongues in their mouths and their dicks in their pants.

We ate once per day at a sit down restaurant similar to a Waffle House or Denny's. Smitty made ridiculous, obscene remarks while we would look at the menu. "I am going to ask the waitress if they serve cumquats here" he would snicker. The cumquat joke was used at almost every restaurant we went to and he did it for the reaction on the waitresses' face as he would slowly say something like, "do you have any beautiful juicy cumquats?" We were all supposed to laugh at this joke. I hated him.

We checked into a different motel, this one with a pool. Like the kid I was, I was anxious to swim and inquired if he'd let me. Smitty and his woman both agreed I could for awhile and they accompanied me to the pool when no one was using it. I watched as an older gentleman made conversation with Smitty over toward the parking area. Smitty was fully dressed and not swimming. Likewise, his woman counterpart also sat in shorts and a top on a lounge chair while I enjoyed the water.

As we returned to the room, my captors decided it was time for a lesson. I was told that if I found myself about to have sex with someone, I needed to know how to check him and make sure he did not have a venereal disease. Smitty and his woman took me into the bathroom and instructed me on how to first clean the guy. This seemed strange and clinical, like something that would happen at the hospital or doctor.

I was visually instructed using Smitty as a model and his woman, as the cleaner, to stroke his penis until you get a dab of preliminary ejaculate and put it on your finger – then touch that finger with your thumb and see if the strand stays together or breaks easily. Also look at the color. They were showing me this to try and determine if the man had a disease. This was sick, sick. Plus, I knew it was not a thorough way to determine if someone had a disease.

We went through the motions with Smitty as the model "John". I could barely keep a straight face for wanting to laugh at the absurdity and awkwardness of the entire situation. It was embarrassing to me, yet I knew if I resisted, I'd be subjected to pain again.

Of course, the entire lesson ended with me having sex with Smitty and he had an obsession with fingering me first and trying to make me have an orgasm or "come" as he constantly called it. I did not know about orgasms and I was extremely uptight. I never experienced pleasurable sensations during these sexual encounters. It was more like I disconnected from the entire experience. I was there, but I wasn't there.

I could have been a dead turkey he was shoving fingers into and watching for some response on my face. But, I felt nothing but uncomfortable sensations and embarrassment. I was so used to stuffing my feelings deep inside and I had extreme control over them.

No, this was more like asking someone to tickle you in your most ticklish places and refusing to flinch or feel it. Controlled by your mind, you would not submit or let go, and you really had no understanding of what reaction they were wanting from you to begin with. He seemed agitated that I would not respond the way he wanted and if I could not have control over anything else around me, I had control over that.

I was made to have sex with a complete stranger a couple of hours later – the same man Smitty had spoke with outdoors while I was swimming. I was instructed to take him into the bathroom of the motel room first and clean his genitalia. Smitty watched as the older man arrived into the room and I silently took him into the bathroom. I heard Smitty move toward the door as well and knew he was just outside listening. We emerged from the bathroom and his "cleaning". I had been instructed to undress and get on top of the man. Smitty sat in a chair in the corner and watched as the old guy quickly gave up what he had. I was completely humiliated. I then retreated back to the bathroom where I cleaned myself repeatedly, crying the whole time.

Smitty and his woman had been quite insistent that I should always be on top of a guy, never underneath him. This was to have more control over the situation if he became violent. It was a strange dichotomy. Smitty could be violent but was concerned that no one else be so. Obviously, I did not want anyone to be violent. Yet, I was smart enough to realize that being on top did not insure I would not be physically hurt. There was to be no kissing of a customer at all. That was fine with me.

One night, the quiet guy with the car that had initially transported us out of state made a reappearance. I did not know where he had been and didn't care. We had actually taken a Greyhound bus from the town he left us in to the one we were in now. They were small towns with small populations. This one was larger than the last and even had taxi cabs which we had taken a couple of times.

I was made to have sex with the other quiet man who had returned. I do not remember his name. Of course, I did not want to have sex with him and he could tell that. We both fell asleep in the same bed where he had used me. During the night, I suddenly sat straight up because I heard my mother yelling for me. I sat there for a moment, making sure I was not dreaming. Again, I heard my mother calling my name. It was very clear and loud. He startled awake and asked what was going on. I told him I hear my mother. I hear her yelling for me. I was convinced she was outside. "Can't you hear her?" I asked.

I think this really spooked him. He knew I was underage and they had been using a fake birth certificate for me to work at the strip clubs. He departed our group the next day, leaving me with the pimp and his woman.

That night, I was forced to have sex with Smitty and the woman. I displayed a strong objection to this happening with the woman and Smitty pulled out his gun, once again, and held it to my head while she raped me. Her first name was the same as my own mother and that felt like another thorn in my side. In my mind, I just referred to her as Smitty's woman -- not wanting to give her a real human existence with her name. I did not hate her. I just wanted to make her invisible. On another level, I felt a bit of compassion for her. It was obvious she had been victimized also, probably at a young age. Now, I hated everything. I felt so shameful from all these sexual escapades. I was not myself anymore. I was something else and I wanted to be anyone else other than me.

It was getting easier to drink the alcohol and pop the pills they would give me. It was an escape from the pain of it all. Still, I cried to go home whenever I had a moment to myself in the bathroom. I was not doing well at the strip clubs. I obviously did not either know or refused to dance right or get the customer's to buy me expensive drinks. I was not making enough money to satisfy Smitty.

A couple of nights later, Smitty and I took a cab from the strip bar to the cheap motel the three of us were staying in. Smitty's woman stayed on to dance and make money. Smitty was not happy that I was an unenthusiastic dancer and felt I could make more in tips than I was bringing in. He expressed this to me and I felt like he was probably going to beat the crap out of me that night and that is why we had left the club early.

But, intervention came. There was a pounding at the door. "Police, open up!" The police were raiding our motel room. I was pretty freaked out because I knew Smitty had a gun and I could just imagine there would be a gun fight like on television. I hid in the bathroom. There was no gunfire exchanged. He opened the motel room door and the police came in and took us away in separate squad cars.

I watched the whirling lights on the two squad cars light up the small motel exterior and could see Smitty in the back of the other car. I felt panicked with the police. I did not know what would happen next. For a moment, I was terrified about being taken away from Smitty. Looking back, I realize what a mind job he had done on me. Obviously, I had experienced a few moments of Stockholm syndrome.

Here is how the police located me: unbeknownst to me, the thin man with wire rim glasses was evidently very disturbed of my insistence that I heard my mother after having sex with him. He drove two hours or more to my house, knocked on the door and told my mother that he had taken me and could tell her where I was. She actually let him in and he allowed her to call the police detectives working on the case. They arrived moments later, took his statement, put him in handcuffs and took him to jail.

If I had not experienced this clairaudience and was so adamant that I could hear my mother calling me, there is no telling what would have happened to me. He probably would not have returned to tell where I was. It is very probable that I would have ended up dead with the way things were going and the people I had become involved with. I was at the beginnings of major sex trafficking. Smitty was a low level player in the field and he probably would have sold me to someone else because I think he felt I was a liability and too much trouble. I am so very lucky that this man made a decision to tell where I was.

Due to the fact that I left willingly, no one would call it a kidnapping. No one considered I had been raped or mistreated. Instead, I was a very bad girl and that is what the police officer who sat me down to question me told me right up front.

I was then taken to a juvenile facility from the police station and locked up in solitary confinement. The cell was cold and hard with nothing really for comfort. I wanted to kill myself that night and seriously contemplated it. The next day, my parents, aunt and uncle came, picked me up and brought me home. It was a very long, quiet ride all the way back home.

Upon returning, it was so good to be home. My room and bed were such a place of safety compared to where I had been, but I would not see that room ever again. My mother told me they were going to take me to the hospital just to have some tests run for pregnancy and such.

We arrived at the hospital, entered the elevator and my father pushed the sixth floor button which said "Psychiatric Unit". At that point, I blacked out. I don't remember arriving into the ward initially. My mind has put a large blank space there. I don't know if I passed out or just mentally blanked it out. I had been through a lot of trauma in the prior weeks and I would later learn there was the possibility I had blanked out many things I did not want to remember.

My first night in the facility was strange. First, I was subjected to a physical, blood and other tests. Then, I was placed in a room that looked like it was the penthouse suite of one of the most expensive hotels. Located at the top of the hospital, it had a wall of floor to ceiling windows that looked out over the city lights. I was locked up again, but now in a luxurious setting.

I had just started my monthly period and they would not allow me to have a tampon saying it was a risk. I was not sure how people kill themselves or hurt others with a tampon, but they did bring a pad – one at a time. I was not allowed many things in this large, luxurious room due to suicide risk and I wondered how they knew I had entertained those thoughts just a short 24 hours earlier. I only stayed in this room one night.

Spending the next three months at the hospital psychiatric unit was actually good for me. I was shielded from predators of any type that I was obviously susceptible to.

Now sixteen years old, I had spent my birthday in the facility. I had to look at everything that had happened leading up to me taking such a bold move as to run away like Pinocchio chasing a dream that turned into a nightmare. I had therapists to talk about what was really going on with me who would listen and not make a judgment one way or another.

The shame I felt around everything was so deep. It was grooved into me like an impression I felt I would never rid myself of. Why, oh why did I allow myself to be in this situation? What was wrong with me? I lived below an overcast sky and I could not see the sun. I could not see that it really wasn't entirely my fault that I left home trying to chase an elusive dream.

When I met with nurses, doctors and therapists, I unconsciously portrayed myself as sunny in disposition and well balanced. It was an act to avoid the real hurt that lay deep inside, the things I just did not want to face, remember or talk about. I was still stuffing my feelings as if I tucked them into an entirely opaque envelope. No one would see them – including myself. I am sure they knew my tactics.

There was individual therapy, art therapy, group therapy with other teens, many of whom had also run away or were caught smoking marijuana. I did not want one single person there my age to know anything about what had happened to me. I cannot emphasize the shame I felt. I would just tell them I was there for running away from home.

There were also adults in another area with more serious mental challenges. Often, we would hear one of them brought in at night and the accompanying screaming and yelling. Soon, they would be put in a straight jacket and shot up with Thorazine. This always happened in a room that was made just for this purpose. Behind the nurse's station was a locked room with a thick glass window where they could see the patient, but the patient could not see them – like a one way mirror. All of us could see the patient if we walked past the nurse's station. It was a bit disturbing. The walls and floor were padded.

To cooperate was the only way to be released and get out of there. You quickly figured out that not cooperating could not only prolong your time there, but possibly put you in the room behind the nurse's station. Everyone was very nice there, however. There was no reason not to assist them in helping you. It was an upscale psychiatric treatment center and I had my own large room where I was not locked in, except for those times when they brought in a patient who was "uncooperative" and had to go to the special room. During those times, we experienced "lock down" where every door would be locked so that we could only hear what was going on and not come out and see anything. Of course, the main door to the rest of the hospital's sixth floor was always locked.

I felt that secretly everyone knew, all my old school friends for sure knew and it would prevent me from reuniting with them in the future. My parents had told me that we were going to be moving and that I would attend a new school on the opposite side of town. While this felt scary, it also felt freeing. Escaping the reality of facing friends' questions and the shame I felt inside was paramount.

While I knew there were things wrong with my mother, she seemed like the sane one and I the crazy. After all, I was the one who ran away. I was the one obsessed with stardom. I was the bad girl and she seemed like a saintly mother who I had done wrong, who I had hurt terribly – enough that I heard her voice calling me clearly two hundred miles away.

A few weeks prior to me being released, my parents were required to attend family therapy with me in hope that we could integrate well together. It was understood that we would continue this therapy weekly once I was released.

Upon leaving the hospital, we moved to a new house my father had built and a new area of town. We were leaving everything that had happened behind. My mom seemed like she was really trying and had taken me out on one trip from the hospital to pick out wallpaper for my new room.

Unfortunately, the family therapy stopped rather abruptly after my release. We had begun addressing me and my issues. We had addressed my father and some of his issues with the family counselor. However, my mom just did not want to look at anything she could be doing different or needed help with. She stood up abruptly one day in the session and announced to the therapist that she was perfect, there was nothing wrong with her, and that she would not be back. She left the room. My father, the therapist and I all just looked at each other stunned. Still, my father made the time for us to try a couple of additional sessions with the therapist, but we all agreed that if we could not address these things with all parties present, it was of very limited use.

I attended a new high school and made several friends. We never talked about what happened to me. I felt shame around all of it. I tried to make friends with girls who were having more normal fifteen and sixteen year old experiences, often feeling like I was tainted and could not live the "goody two shoes" life after my experiences. There were so many things I did remember still that I would never share with another. Pushed down into the crevices of my shame I carried around, I appeared gregarious and sometimes over the top in my outward personality to compensate for what lie underneath.

Years later in conversation with my mother, I asked her if the other man (con artist/pimp) that took me had been convicted. She said no. Charges were not brought against him. This was very disturbing that he had received no punishment for what he had done to me. I wondered who he had victimized next.

She also told me that my father had to go down to the morgue during the time I was missing for body identification purposes. A girl's body had been found that they thought may have been me. I know that must have been terribly traumatic. I really regret bringing all of this upon my family and myself. Lucky to be alive, if I had not heard my mother's voice calling me through some type of clairaudience, that slim, quiet guy would have perhaps not felt the need to flee. He did use this to his advantage, turning himself in and getting out of drug charges he had pending.

I only found these things out years later in my thirties. As I said before, no one wanted to talk about what had happened. We shut the door and it was like we were pretending it did not happen.

It's strange how our memory works. There are so many little details I cannot remember about that time. I found myself waking up some mornings while I worked on this section of the book remembering bits and pieces I had forgotten, despite the fact that it happened so very long ago. I placed them in the chapter, realizing that the details really didn't matter so much – whether we had traveled by car or greyhound bus to different locales. What mattered was the short and long term effect the entire experience had on me – how it made me feel inside. Shame covered me so deep that I had unknowingly added another layer of gunk to walk around in life with. I not only did not want others to know or see it – it needed to stay covered from me as well, like it happened to another girl and not me.

Yet writing this did make me remember more details. It was an unveiling, a revealing for myself and now the world of all that stood collected in me that was vile. I had explored it before during my life, but not to this depth. The writing of the memoir seemed like a driven task that had to be completed before I could go on to write any other books. There was a voice inside that needed to be heard.

Somehow, grace had come my way as I felt a healing take place, an understanding of why I had continued on such a reckless path at different times of my life, devoid of self love.

We stay stuck on a spoke of the wheel of life as the gears of the universe turn around us. We take up with the same sorts of people that have hurt us before. Had I not been so unhappy at home, this would never have happened. Raised by a psychologically afflicted mother, I was easy prey for a predator like Smitty.

Endings and Beginnings

"The greatest stories are those that resonate our beginnings and intuit our endings, our mysterious origins and our numinous destinies, and dissolve them both into one."

-- Ben Okri

My beloved dog, Jacque, and I were extremely close. One could say we had a psychic bond. On the other hand, my first marriage never proved to be quite as strong as the relationship I shared with my canine companion. These two pairings seemed to collide one day in May. It was a time laden with strange and unusual coincidences that brought forth new beginnings and painful endings.

Always happy to see me return home, Jacque was a smart little poodle that had grown up with me since age seven. Champagne in color and miniature in size, he was not quite as "yappy" as the smaller toy versions. He loved to run with me, play chase and do little tricks such as sitting on his hind legs, producing a patty cake motion with his front paws. From a young age, I felt like he allowed me to exercise the circus trainer in me. He seemed to enjoy these antics as much as we loved watching him perform. Jacque loved the attention. We remained close throughout my child and teen years.

Upon leaving the psychiatric section of the hospital, I made a move with my family to the opposite side of the city. I think my parents did this for security reasons and to just start over in some way. This was a financial move up and yet, we did not have nearly the wealth of the neighbors that surrounded us. We imagined our new neighbors aghast as we drove down the street in our old vehicle which often backfired loudly. Giggling at the enormous sound of our car's flatulence, I would shrink down in the backseat to avoid the embarrassment of being seen in what I perceived to be our *"Beverly Hillbillies"* vehicle.

Of course, moving involved changing high schools. It was 1975 and the city had just instituted mandatory bussing for desegregation purposes. On the list of those to be transported far into the city, I was disappointed to not graduate from the neighboring school. I did not imagine myself as prejudiced, having made a very close friend who was racially different from me at the hospital. I did worry about going so far away to school as it was quite a distance. Much unnecessary violence had erupted in our city over the forced desegregation and it was a shame to see grown adults filled with so much hatred fueled by ignorance. The example it set for the children of this time was not good and it affected both sides, black and white.

Once settled into junior year at the inner city school, I made some new friends quickly who did not live too far away. Cindy captured my heart as my new best friend. She had beautiful almond shaped brown eyes with thick curled eyelashes. She loved to wear lipstick and this was unusual for girls our age. The trend at the time was a more natural look with makeup. She had a huge smile and the lipstick she wore set it off in a lovely way. She was always checking her hair and lipstick when she was near a mirror as if to make sure she was still intact.

Cindy's house was not within walking distance but less than a ten minute drive from my home. She lived in a Cape Cod style house with her mother who was a nurse. Cindy came from a large Catholic family with many brothers and sisters. Being the youngest child left at home, she had the entire upstairs of the house as her bedroom. It was very large and she burned incense constantly to cover up the smell of her cigarette smoke upstairs.

I often spent the night with her and felt so free. Her parents were divorced and with her mom being a nurse and working long shifts, we were often completely unsupervised. Cindy drove and had her own car. It was the ugliest station wagon you can imagine – probably one of the first ones ever produced. The seats were torn, and the burgundy paint job on the exterior was worn and had no shine left to it. The important thing was it ran and it was our escape from the school we were not crazy about going to in the first place.

I never told any of my friends what had happened to me just months earlier with Smitty and company. Everyone in our family kept quiet about it. My parents never discussed it with me at all. To not speak about it was to make it something that did not happen in a strange sort of way. Yet, I still carried the trauma and shame. But, I didn't know that on a conscious level.

The high school building was old and in need of considerable repairs. Most of the halls were lined with a dingy yellow subway tile.

Prior to desegregation, this school belonged to the African-American high school teens of that district. Many did not like the white kids invading their space. It seemed that the females were more vocal and bitter about this than the males. I felt I had entered the school with no prejudices that I knew of.

Each day presented new challenges of not feeling anger toward people who obviously didn't like you. I never went to the bathroom alone. White girls were often attacked by black girls in the bathrooms for no reason other than because you were white. This did occur once to me when I had Cindy with me. Luckily, we were able to flee and did not fight back.

I wished we could have all been friendlier that first year, but it was a new situation for everyone. The violence and news headlines left a community atmosphere that brewed hurt and anger under the surface. This was showing itself in many ways with the teens. Going into the second year of desegregation, things began to ease and not be quite as tense between kids coming from two different areas of town, with two different colors of skin. Many of us were even becoming friends.

At least two days a week, Cindy and I would check into home room, maybe go to first and second period and then meet up in the parking lot and take off to a party. These daytime parties consisted of a group of high school kids finding a way to score some beer and pot. In good weather, we would meet up at a local park. We would spend the entire day drinking beer and getting high -- then attempting to return to our houses like normal kids coming home from school. Due to the administrative staff and officials spending most of their time monitoring behavior and breaking up fights, it was easy to cut classes and not be caught or punished.

Occasionally, we would go to another student's house and watch television or sit around and listen to music. It was one of those days at Tom's house that I met my first husband. Tom attended another school and seemed to have frequent day parties. I went there only one time and struck up a conversation with a guy named Adam. It was not a flirty conversation, but I must have made some impression on him. A few days later, Adam sent word through other students that he wanted to ask me out. I asked a lot of questions about him. What did everyone know about him? They told me he was soon graduating and going to attend the University. Adam worked at a local grocery store and had a vehicle. I drove at the time, but only my mother's car and usually for trips to the store for her.

Adam took me on nice dates and had money to spend on a 16 year old girl. He was extremely responsible and had not one, but two cars - his Mustang he drove daily and a 1956 Jaguar that was a garage kept, weekend car. The garage was actually in another part of town that he rented for the Jag. The entire time we dated and were married, I never rode once in the Jaguar. It had many little mechanical issues and never seemed to run with ease. When we divorced, he seemed concerned about his garage asset and I told him, "Don't worry, you can keep that Jaguar. It was yours to begin with and besides, it never runs." He did keep both of his cars.

Dating a college guy, I attended quite a few formal fraternity dances and loved getting dressed up for these events. It was sometime during the first year of dating that Adam and I moved into a sexual relationship with each other. I was concerned about becoming pregnant and made an appointment with my mother's gynecologist to get some type of birth control. I asked the doctor to please not tell my mother I had come there. I worked a part-time job and had some money to cover these costs on my own. Instead of paying at the desk upon leaving, the staff person told me a bill would be sent to me. I worried about that but since I picked up the mail each day on the way inside from school. I planned on intercepting the bill.

Adam and I often would get a room at the local Howard Johnson motel and we felt very private there together. By now, I was seventeen and the year was 1976. I liked dating a college guy. There were no guys at my school I was interested in. They all seemed as trapped and helpless as I felt.

In November of 1976, I missed getting the mail and my mother found the bill. She ransacked my belongings in my room, finally finding the birth control pills in my purse after I came home. In the kitchen, she flew into a rage over it. "You're nothing but a slut!" she yelled, waving the pill packet in the air. "You are nothing but a little whore" she went on. My mother destroyed that packet and two others I had for upcoming months, throwing them in the garbage. She went on, "I cannot believe you went to *my* doctor for these. I am so embarrassed." I sat on the green bench in the kitchen with tears streaming down my face looking at the floor. I said nothing to her and finally just walked upstairs to my room and locked the door.

Words like whore and slut cut deep into me emotionally as they paralleled the shame I carried from my time with Smitty. Was this why we never talked about it? I am ruined; a whore and no one can change the past or make me anything but dirty. Children who are victims of sexual abuse often carry a layer of sludge they feel can never be washed off.

My mom was pregnant at the time. I chose not to get her any further upset, but I was torn to pieces on the inside. I was trying to be responsible by getting the pills. Her calling me these names touched the core of shame I carried with me. Yes, there was a part of me that felt like a used up whore instead of a seventeen year old sexually active girl with a boyfriend.

I loved music and took great pleasure in picking up a new album each time I was paid from my part-time job. The most popular music within my peer group would be bands like Led Zeppelin, Fleetwood Mac, Pink Floyd, Queen, Yes, and Aerosmith. I'm probably leaving out some important artists here, but just to give you the flavor of the rock music we were into. I also listened to a lot of pop, Motown and individual artists like Joni Mitchell.

Later in December of 1976, I was upstairs in my room listening to a new Joni Mitchell album, *"Hejira"*. The fretless bass combined with Joni's voice and thoughtful poetry created a magical mood in me. My mother called to me from the kitchen that I had a phone call. I expected it to be Adam or maybe one of the girls from school. I ran downstairs and asked my mom, "Who is it?" She replied, "Some old woman."

I took the corded phone from her hand and said "Hello." Truly, an old woman's voice was on the phone. She said, "Is this Lyra?" "Yes", I said. "Who is this?" The old woman replied, "I can't tell you who I am, but I need you to listen to me. I am calling to warn you about something. I don't want you to be afraid, but I need to give you a warning." "Who is this?" I demanded in a stronger tone. My mother looked at me as I spoke. She was curious about the call.

The old woman continued, "Look child, I am trying to help you. Something terrible is going to happen to you and your family on the thirteenth of January. Something is going to happen that will completely change your life. There is more that I need to tell you, but I can't right now. I will call you again with further instructions for you. Again, I am not trying to scare you, just help." The telephone went silent. I looked at my mom and told her the conversation.

The entire time the old woman spoke, my brain was scanning itself like it had engaged into its sound database to find who I knew that could disguise their voice like that. I just could not imagine which of my friends could have done this. I thought about everyone our family knew. I could come up with no answer and decided this was some sort of prank, yet there remained a nagging feeling that this was no hoax. She knew my name. She said the 13th of January. Her voice was more haunting than Joni's on her mysterious new album. I turned my stereo off when I returned upstairs.

The call and the old woman's voice continued to bother me the next day at school. I had committed the resonance of her voice to my memory. It was early morning and school had not yet begun. As several of my friends sat smoking in the girl's bathroom, I leaned quietly against the wall wondering which one of these girls could have made the call. Listening to them rattle their tales with one another, there wasn't a single one in the group that I could say certain may have done this.

The old woman's voice on the phone sounded aged. There was a texture to it that would be hard to fake. Still, just in case, I didn't mention the call to any of them. I felt mad and I just wanted to say, "Which one of you did this?" I wanted someone to blame for that crazy call.

After a few days, I forgot about the phone call, returning to life as usual, anxious for Christmas and the holidays. The New Year came and we celebrated ending 1976 and welcoming 1977. Adam and I continued to date during this time and have our regular motel sessions after a dance or date.

On January 12th, I arrived home from school. Normally, my mom would be in the kitchen or perhaps doing something in the living room. Instead, she was not in sight. My dad, who would normally not be at home at this time, was sitting quietly in a chair. We greeted each other and he went on to tell me that something was wrong with the baby inside my mother who was now eight and a half months into her pregnancy. He said they found it through ultrasound and that tomorrow she would be having a cesarean section and the baby would be removed.

I asked him, "Then, what?" My father explained that the baby suffered anencephaly, meaning it was missing all or enough portions of its brain that it would not be able to live on its own. He said the doctors did not expect the baby to survive even though it was already full term in size. I felt so bad for my mother. How could she deal with having a child growing inside for over eight months only to have it removed and then she has no baby?

On January 13th, the baby was born, lived a very short time and died. My father made burial arrangements. We never had any family ceremony or closure. Our house was silent as my mother returned home from the hospital. I am sure that I did not do enough to help or console her. Dad told me it had been a girl.

There is more pain in this situation my mother endured. Years later, she told me that there had been protestors outside the hospital when she was admitted and during her stay. These protestors were accusing my mother of having an abortion and calling it murder. Someone at the hospital had breached patient confidentiality. It seemed to point at the staff, although no one could ascertain it directly. A doctor, who was not her physician, came in to see her prior to the birth pleading with her not to do this, saying it was inhumane and murder.

Due to the volatile climate, her own obstetricians chose to try and let her give birth naturally at eight and a half months pregnant and began a drip to induce labor. She labored for hours with the baby she knew did not even have all the body parts to live on its own, only ending up with a c-section once enough time had passed that met the hospital's standards of practice. She also said the nurses treated her very poorly compared to when she had given birth to any of her other children.

Obviously, the phone call from the old woman had entered my mind several times during this family situation. Was it just a huge coincidence that this all happened on the 13th of the next month, just as she had predicted? I did not bring up the subject with my mother. I really did not know what to say to her except that I was so sorry she went through this. The old woman had stated she would call again to give me instructions on what to do. What could I have done to change these circumstances? To my knowledge, she had never called again.

Valentine's Day came, but my monthly cycle did not. I soon determined I was pregnant and spent some days in denial about it. Perhaps if I just forgot about it like other things, it wouldn't be there – wouldn't be real. But it was real, along with nausea in the morning. I finally told Adam about it. Now, we could be worried together. Abortion was legal and I explored that as an option along with adoption. I could not embrace these solutions for my situation at the time.

I was now pregnant at seventeen, in my last year of high school and it was time to make some decisions. Once my parents found out, they offered to allow me to stay with them, have the child and go on to college with them raising it. I didn't feel comfortable with that and I also felt the tug that my child needed a traditional family with a mom and dad raising it and not grandparents. I could not imagine allowing my mom to raise my child due to her outbursts.

Adam had agreed for us to marry. I knew he felt great fear about it. Being underage, I asked my family to sign the papers so that we could get a marriage license. My mother would not oblige. Finally, after much discussion with my dad, he reluctantly agreed and signed the document for us to marry.

Adam and I traveled to Tennessee where we married in the courthouse of a very small town. We then traveled to Gatlinburg, Tennessee for our honeymoon. It was Memorial Day weekend.

I believe it was our second night at the Reagan Motel in the heart of the mountain city that I had a dream about my dog, Jacque. It was disturbing, yet I could not remember all of the details. I had an inner knowing that something was wrong with my Jacque. I asked Adam if I could call home. He was worried about the motel's long distance charges.

With a sense of urgency, I pleaded with him telling him I *knew* something was wrong with my dog. Now for you who are younger, it was a large expense to make long distance calls in those days. We did not have caller identification or cell phones. We were lucky to have push button phones instead of rotary dial.

Adam relented and I called. My mother answered the phone. I told her why I was calling. She confirmed that something had happened. Jacque was outside and some neighbors were shooting off fireworks. It startled him and he ran down the street eventually getting hit by a car. She said that the man who hit him had been kind enough to take him to the nearest veterinarian which happened to be the same vet Jacque went to. Jacque was alive and home now recovering. My heart sank to hear this news, but I was relieved he was alive.

Adam and I lived the first few months of our marriage in my room at my parent's home. As we returned from our honeymoon, I found Jacque lying on the laundry room floor with his injuries. As I petted and loved on him, I was careful to be gentle not knowing how much pain he had. He was taking antibiotics, yet his leg became infected and he died a few days after our return.

We buried him in a wooden box my father constructed for him in the backyard. My little sister actually placed his lifeless body in the box along with his appurtenances. I have always missed this dog and the bond we had. I have loved many dogs since then, but no other could replace him.

My high school graduation ceremony occurred at this time also. It was like all important dates had compacted into one big May event. My mother refused to attend my graduation. I am not sure why. It stung me. Perhaps, it lost all validity for her since I had become pregnant. I was barely showing and would have on a large, flowing graduation gown.

My dad did attend and gifted me with a camera. The loss of my dog, getting married, graduating, adjusting to being pregnant and all of the body changes that were happening to me seemed a bit much looking back. Somehow, I processed and worked through it all. I'm sure I was stuffing my feelings along the way and trying to put on a happy face about it all. Yet, I was excited. I had looked at my options. I could have aborted the baby, consented to adoption, gone on to college and let my parents raise the child. That last option was not going to happen. As I connected with this little one growing inside me, I became more excited each week.

My due date was October 15th. My labor began early in the morning and went all day and night of the 12th. Shortly after midnight on October 13th, I gave birth to a gorgeous, healthy girl. This was such a life changing event. Upon our arrival home from the hospital, my parent's fell in love with this baby as much as I had. Mom helped prepare bottles, change diapers and take over for me at night when she knew I needed rest. She had not been happy about me becoming pregnant, yet the new baby girl had a way of making everything alright in the world, just by her beautiful presence.

One afternoon as I visited with my mom privately in her bedroom, we spoke about the phone call from the old woman the previous December and her warning of something tragic happening to our family the next month on the 13th. Indeed, that was the day my baby sister was born and died. We spoke about the fact that this baby was born nine months later on the 13th of October.

My mother and I exchanged a look of understanding with each other. I felt some strange fate had carved out life directions for us. I passed her new granddaughter to her arms and told her how sorry I was that I did not say or do more for her during that time of her loss. The new grandbaby seemed to fill a void for her and we both cried tears of happiness, as well as sorrow, for all that had transpired.

Often I have pondered these events, the old woman's prediction and the synchronicities. My daughter was born ten months after the lady's phone call warning me of "something that would change my whole life". Many possibilities soared through my mind as one child would be born and die almost immediately. The other child would be born 9 months later. Additionally, the death and birth happening on the same numeral (13) of the month seemed to be like a signature the universe was leaving.

When we think of a human being created, we know it begins with ovum and sperm. To break it down further, there is the DNA. Science today has proven that DNA begins with a wave that exists as a pattern in time and space imprinted upon the universe. It does not initially exist as a molecule. This intelligent wave then gathers the atoms to it that will give it a somewhat ethereal (my definition) form substance to manifest in our reality.

I did not know that information in 1977. In 2017, we hardly understand it all now. I can tell you that, intuitively, I felt that the soul of the baby had jumped from one mother to another, as if there was an unknown reason and this was fate.

Could the dream I had and the horrible, distressed feelings I experienced about my pet when I awoke be a coincidence? Perhaps I just missed my dog? No, I was on my honeymoon. I was away from my parents for goodness sakes – a seventeen year old playing grown up. I can say with absolute certainty that the dream was there because on some level, everything is connected. I was close to this dog and his discomfort was mine.

We are all connected through some invisible source that permeates everything down to levels beyond the sub-atomic. We don't fully understand it here on earth and we may never. But it is there, nonetheless, running like an operating system in the background of our existence. We are all characters in a program lining up and forming the basis of all the information the system holds. Perhaps at rare times, we gain access to another file on the system and can read what is contained therein. Perhaps, a virus or some anomaly is present and must be cleaned up. Whatever the case, there does appear to be a cosmic order to all happenings and what we sometimes think is choice, may be nothing more than acting out the next step in a grandly designed plan.

If this hypothesis is true, we need not try to be Gods with our sciences or rule makers with our religions, we merely need to connect with what forms naturally around us and is not intervened or tampered with by humans.

The word, hejira, means a journey, usually to a better place. The song on Joni Mitchell's album I was listening to at the time of the old woman's phone call was written on a road trip by Ms. Mitchell from the east to west coast of the United States. It has been a long time since I listened to the song *Hejira*. So, I played it while writing portions of this chapter, just to try and recreate the same feelings I had at seventeen. But, it didn't work. It just wasn't there … until I slowly read the words of the song. In it, Joni speaks of death and birth, life purpose and how we are all small parts of the whole.

I played the rhythmic song again, listening closer to the words and releasing my focus on the instrumentation. I paced my office, half singing; the words barely coming off my lips. I stared at all the pictures of my children sitting high atop the credenza. Tears rolled down my cheeks. The web of life appeared right there in front of me. The synchronicity had fired again and was alive as if it never ended.

Becoming a mother began a different journey for me – the most important one I would embark on in my life. Each of my children in their own unique ways have gifted me with knowing them and I feel a deep gratitude for having them in my life that nothing else could replace. Often, I think they believe I molded them into the adults they are today. The fact is they molded me. They stretched me in ways I needed to grow and they taught me how miraculous love is.

The Ambulance

"A dreamer is one who can only find his way by moonlight, and his punishment is that he sees the dawn before the rest of the world."
~ Oscar Wilde

What are the things that come together to create the incredible synchronicities in our lives? There seems to be some sort of magic going on in the background. We cannot anticipate when it will happen or if. It occurs in a series of coordinated events that we did not orchestrate, at least at a conscious level. One question, always present is: do we have some method or ability to help bring it all about? I believe we do. A first step is to live more intuitively and open ourselves to all the signals that can be presented as we attract synchronicity. Yet, the presentation of synchronicity is that it climbs upon our backs, sneaking up on us, coming in from left field without warning. Always, it appears to happen beyond chance.

In the summer of 1982, I received a letter from my ex-husband. I do not remember the contents. Living in another city not too far away, he was probably sending a cordial note along with a child support check because he was and is a very nice person. "Nice" was something I was not looking for in a partner, but I didn't know that at the time. As a girl below the age of twenty, already married and divorced and having still not processed many things from the past effectively, I was attracted more to bad boy types.

The night I received the letter, I dreamed an ambulance brought my former husband, Adam, to me. His hand was bleeding profusely and his fingers were partially cut off. The ambulance would not take him to the hospital. I could not understand why they would bring him to me. He seemed to want to refuse medical care, but I took him to the hospital myself as the ambulance stood idle in front of my house.

The dream was very real and vivid. It haunted me the next day at work. I fretted and fought with myself wondering if I should call him and give him some type of warning, letting him know that I felt something might happen to him or his hand. However, he was more logically oriented and I was afraid he would think I was crazy. Two days later, I called his mother who I had remained good friends with. She informed me that Adam had been in a car accident that day. The damage he sustained was to one of his hands. A truck had run a red light and hit him broadside.

From that point forward, I made a deal with myself to not worry about what other people think. If I have a dream that seems like a very vivid premonition, I must let them know. This has resulted in me swallowing my pride and making that call to someone, letting them know what I feel they need to be aware or cautious of. If I am wrong, no harm done. If I am right, much harm might be avoided.

Perhaps today in the 21st century, you would not hesitate to call someone and warn them about a dream you had. It was uncommon in my circles. While I was very much into metaphysical and spiritual pursuits, it was kept toned down, almost underground. I would only talk about these ideas and thoughts with a few select people.

In many parts of the industrialized world, it is taboo to admit you are psychic. Someone in an indigenous community would perhaps be elevated in social status with these gifts. Someone in a metropolitan city may be laughed at or mocked. Indigenous people live close to and within nature. People in cities have to try and find a spot that contains nature such as a park. It is easier to not be in tune in the city, yet that can be achieved also because there is no barrier to your ability except that which you allow or construct.

We have so much history lending credence to the fact that prophetic ways are real, yet we fear them. We are still living in the dark ages when it comes to things we currently term as paranormal. In the future, these events or happenings will take their place in everyday common normalcy and humans will thrive because of it.

It stands to reason that Jung happened upon synchronicity from working so much with patients' dreams which often could have been precognitive. What if time/space already has all the information in it of what has happened and what will, or the probability of outcomes? It could be that some portion of our consciousness is seeing that major event and desires to alter it in some way with warning us.

Can precognitive warnings assist us in changing the time/space story? If I receive a dream that my dog will be hit by a vehicle on a snowy day when she gets loose, do I not make sure to have a firm grip on her leash and take her out myself each day it snows? Do I prevent the event or do I get hit by a car along with my dog? Does this sound like an old Twilight Zone episode question? Certainly, it does.

Looking at any of the possibilities, it is only fair to examine things from the aspect of fate: an event that is preordained and will happen. In the event that it is fatalistic, this does make it causal as someone or something is causing the event to occur, even if we cannot identify who or what it is.

For the sake of argument, let us assume that everything is fated (which I do not believe it is). If that is the case, maybe synchronicity is like little memory ripples that let you know you are connected to something controlling your fate. Perhaps it is you controlling your fate from a different dimensional level and here is the part where you said, I'm going to give myself a heads up here so that I can allow myself to know that there is something major going on and provide a shock absorber.

Yet fate and destiny are different. Fate is what happens to us that we felt we had no control over. Destiny is you and I deciding how we will let that event shape us. Destiny is a journey – just like hejira. We take from the trip what we make most important to us. We can consciously allow our mistakes, lessons and misfortunes to turn into something golden when we look for the good – searching for any gift that can come from the experience, no matter how difficult that can seem.

We really do not know what we can change about the timeline we experience as life. However, I have heard so many stories from people about how they had a precognitive dream of warning, heeded that information and were able to avoid a situation or disaster. I have also heard stories of people who received warnings and did not heed the information, only to go through something traumatic or changing in their circumstances.

Many people tend to discount dreams yet they hold clues for us to our worries, concerns, solutions and often, the future. Aboriginals believe this waking life we think is real is the dream and that when we sleep, we go back to reality. They call our waking life here on the planet the "dreamtime".

Speaking of dreams, visions, clairaudience and other sixth sensory happenings in an open way with each other could lead us to more discovery and answers. While this is happening with more frequency in our modern societies, it is still frowned on at times and given a multitude of labels.

Yet, when I think of the story my grandfather told of hearing the voice saying stop right now and do not go further, I have to believe that the timeline can be changed by listening to the intuitive sides of our nature and paying attention to our dreams. Often, we hear of people who were killed in a freak car accident. Did they have warnings they did not give any credence? Was there something that happened that told them, go another way or don't go at all? Were these the people that had intuitive urgings or synchronicities and did not heed the message? We will never know unless they had imparted this knowledge to someone else prior to the event.

By listening to the stories of people who did take heed, we can get glimpses into what can be achieved as humans striving to alter what may seem like fate to us. If we have a built-in ability to dodge misfortune by tuning into ourselves and giving that voice more credence, this new reliance should be taught to us from early childhood to young adulthood.

A Sacrifice

"Children and mothers never truly part, bound together
by the beating of one another's heart."
~ Charlotte Gray

In 1980, I took a new job and fell in love with my boss. He was full of the energy you see in someone who has been thoroughly trained in hard core sales. Charismatic and good looking, he told everyone he was separated from his wife, just not yet divorced. Falling for your boss is never wise and more foolish when they are still married.

We moved into an apartment together along with my daughter. Months later, I became pregnant. It soon became clear that, even though he was not living with his wife and the three children he already had, he was not going to marry me or support the pregnancy. By this time, I could already see he had little money to contribute to our bills after paying money to his current wife. It became apparent that I had been nothing more than a fun diversion for this man and he wanted no part of making things permanent.

He moved out of the apartment, staying at times with one of his buddies and other nights with his wife as they would go through some strange back and forth dance of a relationship. My financial woes continued and I ended up losing my car after failing to make payments on it. The rent was way past due and finally, I had nowhere to live.

This is what can happen when you are not loving yourself and making better choices. You are looking for someone outside of yourself to fulfill this part of you that is a gaping hole and you attract the wrong relationships.

My daughter and I had very little food. I existed on enriched white rice with canned tomatoes mixed in. I had little resources to draw upon and I was afraid to tell my parents just how dire things were. To me, this would have resulted in more lectures from my father and my mother screaming what a piece of shit I was.

Circumstances made me feel I could not keep this child due to money. It really became about cash flow of which I had none. I decided that I had to give this baby up for adoption. I also wanted the child's parents to have money. I did not want this little one to ever want for anything since it would be missing its birth parents. I was so focused on what I did not possess that I wanted to make sure this child never went without it.

I found an excellent attorney who did private adoptions. Taking a bus to his office in the city, he met with me and explained how the adoption process worked. I would be given complete profiles of potential parents to choose from with all details about them such as race, religion, occupations, net worth, etc. Of course, I would never know their name or address. I would be required to fill out an extensive questionnaire about health, not just mine, but for the father and our extended families. I completed all of the paperwork for my family's side and the father's as best as possible and mailed it back to his office.

The attorney called to say he had some possible couples and that he wanted to meet with me. Again, I jumped on a city bus and made my way to his office with my three year old daughter along. I read the profile of the parents, their net worth, industries they were in, etc. He told me they would pay for all my medical expenses and give me money for my rent, utilities and food each month. I chose a particular couple whose profile I liked the most. They were millionaires.

I rented a one bedroom apartment in a rough area of town. It was cheap and on the bus line. I spent my days there with my daughter and lived out this pregnancy which was a very healthy one, yet had this anticipated hard end looming over it. When it came time for me to have the baby, I let my parents know as they had requested. My old school friend, Cindy, took me to the hospital.

My doctor was fantastic and it was a fairly easy birth to a baby girl. The hospital separated me on another floor from the other new mothers. I am sure this was protocol with an adoption situation. I recovered in bed watching Princess Diana's royal wedding on television. It all looked so fairytale dreamy and I felt so bad for myself. Many girls fantasize or expect that they would have a beautiful wedding and I could not see that in my future. At such a tender young age I felt like my chances for anything of that sort were long gone. I drowned myself with postpartum pity and really felt sorry that I had made such a mess of my life thus far.

I told one of the nurses that I wanted to go down to the nursery and see my child. I had only been able to see her very briefly at the birth. She strongly urged me not to, advising it was not good. However, legally they could not keep me from doing so. I held my baby girl and fed her a bottle, noticing all the features of her face, hands and such. She was just beautiful and it bothered me that she would not receive round the clock mothering from me.

Returning to my hospital room, I broke down and bawled. It was so very hard not to leave the hospital with my baby. I cried almost non-stop. I never knew I could feel grief that intense. My doctor came in at one crying session and told me that I could keep her if I wanted. I told him I knew that, but I have promised this couple and they are counting on me. They have been paying the bills. He told me not to worry about that and his bill could be paid back slowly over time to him. Deep down, I just felt like I had to keep the commitment I had made.

I left the hospital and went back home, with my little girl arriving who had stayed with relatives during my hospitalization. I would receive one more rent check during my postpartum period and then I would need to get back to work. Finding a job was on my mind, but not my first worry.

I began having symptoms of a heart attack at night. I was not overweight and only 21 years old. I phoned my doctor's emergency number and he called back. I told him about my pain and where it was located. He said, "You can go to the hospital if you want, but I think you are just feeling a lot of anxiety and stress from this. Do go and get checked out though".

I didn't go, but the intense chest pains continued on and off nightly. I was literally heartbroken. Each night as I lie in bed, I would start to fall asleep only to be awakened by excruciating and debilitating chest pains. My baby was still at the hospital. Why had she not been united with her new parents?

A couple of days later, my attorney phoned me to say that he and his wife were personally boarding a plane with the baby to take her to California to her new home. He also explained to me again that she would have a California birth certificate from the documents we had agreed upon and signed, instead of one from my home state.

That evening, my chest pains did not return. I felt calmer and more at peace. I actually felt a bit joyful and relieved. The next morning, I received a phone call from my attorney and he said, "I want to let you know she is with her new parents and the new mother would like to speak to you, is that okay?" I told him yes. He passed the phone to her and she was elated, crying joyfully about how happy they were and thanking me. I really don't remember what I said to her in response. I was crying as well. You could truly hear the gratitude in this lady's voice and the choice, though almost impossible to make, felt right.

I believe the cessation in my chest pains and anxiety ended because my baby was finally with her new family. Surely, there can be that type of bond between a mother and her child.

Of course, I had not been allowed to know who the parents were. However, I desperately wanted to know. I prayed one night telling God that if he would allow me to know, I would never abuse that information and contact them, but that I had to know for my own peace of mind. Even though I had spoke with the new mother and things all seemed legitimate, I feared that I had been conned out of my baby and something devious could have happened to her.

A few days later, I went to the attorney's office to pick up my last household expense check. The secretary gave it to me by accident in the Federal Express envelope it had arrived in. Always, it would be drawn on the escrow account of the new parents' attorney in California so I could never tell from the check who the parents were. However, on the outside of the envelope on the Fed Ex bill of lading it had their last name. I was able to take the last name on the envelope and do a little research.

I went straight to the large public library in the city with my little girl. I took her to the children's area and we chose some books for her. She accompanied me with her reading material to the research area of the main library. Beginning at Who's Who, I was quickly able to determine the parents' identity. I knew their ages, religion, and approximate income. I knew that he was in the movie industry and she had her own career as a fashion designer. I knew they had a boy of age five that was also adopted. I liked this fact when I chose them because my child would have an older sibling. Plus, it was not their first rodeo having a child. I kept my promise and I have never contacted them.

These synchronicities: my severe chest pain disappearing when my baby girl was united with her new parents. My prayer was answered when the secretary gave me the entire envelope by accident with the adoptive parents' last name on it. This gave me the peace of mind I needed to go forward with my life.

I decided I needed a different type of job. Going through the want ads for other ideas besides food service, I knew how to type from high school. With no experience, I interviewed as a legal secretary in a small law office with two attorneys. They did say they had a lot of applicants and it seemed they would have a hard time making a decision. The position did not pay very much, but it would be something I knew I could learn quickly and maybe move up to a larger salary soon. After the interview, I didn't hesitate. I picked up the phone, called one of the attorneys and told him, "I really want this job." They gave it to me. I knew nothing but I was smart and figured things out fast.

As far as the adoption was concerned, this just became another thing no one in my family spoke about. On holidays or other occasions when I saw them, no one said a word. They probably wondered if it would embarrass me and it could have. Inside, I felt like the really screwed up offspring in the family --- someone who had created a mess of the family tree. A new layer of shame had merged atop the one already there.

The Magic of Unicorns

"In the universe there is an immeasurable, indescribable force which shamans call intent, and absolutely everything that exists in the entire cosmos is attached to intent by a connecting link."
~ *Carlos Castaneda*

I learned the legal business quickly, along with preparing pleadings and other related documents for the two attorneys. In the beginning, I was a mess in trying to figure out the legal jargon. There was much emphasis on what was an original document and a copy and I had to keep that straight. I found it easier to make sure original documents were on a thicker grade of paper, as the copies would be thinner. If the clients would use blue ink instead of black, that was helpful also.

No one was using computers yet to prepare all these documents. I first began on an old electric typewriter and white correction fluid was always nearby. I later talked the attorneys into purchasing a new electronic typewriter. This one had memory and tape that had a self-correcting feature. The stored memory feature made things easier as so many legal documents begin and end with repetitive phrases.

I found a place for my little girl to stay during work hours where she received great child care and the fees were income based. This helped and I was starting to accept the idea of being on my own, without a partner. I moved to a nicer area of town and began pursuing things that interested me. Thanks to my grandparents, I had a car now too. It was old and had its issues, but I was delighted to have wheels.

After working for those two attorneys for a little over a year, I decided to apply to a larger law firm where I could get a salary raise. I did get the job. It was short-lived. I jumped too soon into a very large law firm and the attorney I worked for was a real stickler about being on time to work. I was often ten or fifteen minutes late. My car that my grandparents had given me had a lot of problems starting, especially on cold mornings. This created more tardiness. Although I always stayed longer to make up for the time, that did not seem to matter to my boss.

As he readied himself for vacation one week, he piled on the work. He literally dictated fifty full length back and front tapes full of pleadings and letters. He had them all attached to their reciprocal files and stacked in piles. They made a wall three to four feet tall around my desk. He stated that all of the work must be completed before he left for vacation. I got the message. He wanted to overwhelm me and hope that I quit. Of course, with no other job to go to and my dire finances, I could not do that. I tried my best to get through the work and another older secretary next to me helped also when she had any spare time. She knew what was going down and could not believe the amount of work he had piled upon me. Staying late, skipping lunches and, with her help, I made it through the wall of dictated documents.

Once he returned from vacation, he called me into his office. Written up for my tardiness numerous times in the past was enough justification for him to boot me out of the position. That is the first time I was ever fired from a job. It was a blow to my ego and my finances.

Worried now about my resume, I felt I had better find different work once again. I feared that if I applied for a secretarial position and it showed I had been fired, I would be wasting my time and just embarrassing myself. One of my friends worked in sales for an office machine company and I applied with the company at her invitation. After taking a battery of tests, I was hired for the job. The training was not so great and I really was not prepared for this job either. I cannot say I was fired, but I struggled to stay there and eventually quit. I was not making enough sales and saw my low performance as failure.

Sales would eventually be something I was very good at in life. Yet, my position required that I confidently walk into the offices of doctors and executives, make convincing presentations to win their business, and sell them machines. Some days, depending upon how I felt about myself, it was quite difficult to do the footwork. I was walking around feeling not worthy or good enough to approach these people that had a higher social standing. On many occasions, I remember arriving at various offices in my car and just being frozen there, afraid to walk inside. There were other days when I felt more confident or at least psychologically pumped myself up to make the contact and try to get a sell.

During my sales job, I saw an advertisement in the newspaper for a singer in a local band and called to inquire. The band leader I spoke with described the music they performed and gave me a list of five songs to learn and what night to show up to audition. Each night after work, I would practice the songs in my apartment, probably driving the guy downstairs crazy.

I cinched the audition and now had another way of making cash on the weekends with this band. While most of the gigs were in our own city, we also covered a radius that reached into Ohio and other parts of our own state. This side job allowed me to make at least another hundred dollars per week – often more. Best of all, it was doing something I always wanted to do.

I loved being in the band and it was my desire above all to do this for a living. I was still young and having a child did make it difficult. I would take her to my parent's or another relative on weekends when the band was performing. I felt that being on stage and singing would be the most fantastic thing to do in life. The applause, the people, even if on a small scale had captured me.

I was also aware that to make a real living at such an endeavor, I would need to have some sort of big break. I was not in a position to move to California or even Nashville. Yet, I daydreamed frequently about living the life of stardom. Performing with my new band had given me a lot of confidence that had been shriveled by past events.

In February 1983, Tom Petty and The Heartbreakers were going to be in concert at the Louisville Gardens. One of the songs we performed in our band was *Stop Draggin' My Heart Around* featuring Tom and Stevie Nicks, another musician I dearly loved. I became filled with crazy, pure intent.

Somehow, I got it in my mind that I could leap ahead with my music career if I could convince Tom Petty to let me sing that song with him at the concert. Stevie wasn't going to be there, so I knew if I practiced enough, I could pull it off.

The weekend job with the band had assisted me in rekindling my ideas of being a star again. To have this kind of adoration was something I thought would give me validation, make me feel loved and worthy. Blind to everything, trying to get a break by singing on stage with Tom Petty consumed me day and night.

Reading an in-depth article several times about Tom in a national rock magazine, I felt like I knew him personally. He seemed so genuine and down to earth in the well written piece. I pulled out my best stationary that sported a beautiful blue unicorn on it and started writing Tom a very heartfelt letter. It must have been at least four pages long. I sealed it in a matching unicorn envelope, putting a lot of mental intention inside.

In the letter, I told Tom about all my jobs I had worked and, like him, I had been fired a couple of times. I told him about my band and who our local agent was. I let Tom know that, more than anything, I would like to sing his duet with him since Stevie was not going to be able to make it.

I drove to the venue the day of the show with letter in hand. Although I was able to get into the exterior front doors, the set of interior doors were chained shut. I watched all the roadies setting up through a small window. They were very far away from the inner vestibule area. Finally, a guy noticed me and came over to the door. He was able to open the door just enough with the chains to hear me and for me to pass something through the small opening.

I told him I had a letter that just had to get to Tom Petty right away. He said he would make certain he got it. I said "Really, don't just say that. This is important. You must get that letter in his hands." He promised he would and said, "Look, he's staying at the Hyatt. I'm headed over there myself later and I will make sure he gets it. You should come over there and meet me and the crew. We will be at the bar in the lobby later." I thanked him and left.

My daughter was at my parent's house and I went back to my apartment to get ready for something …. I did not know what for sure. As you can imagine, I had a difficult time knowing what to wear for the event. I did not have tickets to the show, but I was so hoping I could sing with Tom, that would not be an issue at that point. Following the roadie's invite, I decided to go down to the hotel just in case that led to something happening, such as a meeting with Tom Petty.

Wearing the most expensive dress I owned, it was black silk with a very small floral print on it and sort of "gypsy" looking. My ensemble was nothing as detailed as Stevie would wear, but it would have to work. I put the cassette tape of Tom Petty & The

Heartbreakers in my car's deck and sang all the way to the Hyatt, imagining myself with the band.

Parking in the hotel garage, I made my way inside to a large circular bar at the base of the open atrium of the hotel. The guy who had promised to get the letter to Tom was present, along with other support staff for the band. There were some very beautiful women sitting around the bar and you could tell they were not local. With chiseled high cheekbones and bodies of models, they were gorgeous. I was pretty. Momentarily, I started my not feeling good enough routine inside my brain. I pulled it together and did not let that stop me. This was not a beauty contest. This was about a break, a chance at singing.

My new roadie friend introduced himself and we sat having a drink. Finally he asked "So, what's in the letter?" I told him my crazy idea about singing with Tom and he smiled. "Well, you never know!" he said. I could tell he thought I was just a crazy, star struck person – and he was right. He told me that he had been a guitar player in Alice Cooper's band and I was not sure I believed him. By this time, I knew people might tell you most anything. Now, Alice's band had broken up in the 1970's and maybe he had. Perhaps, he was picking up extra money working as a roadie. Later, I confirmed he did do this by finding an old Alice Cooper album. He looked a little older now and his hair was now short instead of long.

I could tell he had taken a liking to me and I ignored that. I had no interest in getting hooked up with someone who would be leaving town tomorrow. My aim was very clear. This was not about romance; it was about a chance at something big that would possibly change my world. Time was slipping away and the show started in a couple of hours. Two glasses of white wine down, I did not want to get too tipsy. Feeling pulled by my intuition, I mentioned that I felt I should go over to the backstage door now and see if I could get in. He offered to go along and I agreed thinking he might be able to help me since he was "with the band".

I vividly remember waiting in a short line of cars to exit the Hyatt parking garage. While in line, my new roadie friend told me that he didn't want me to be upset but that I was probably not going to get to talk to Tom Petty. I said, "Yeah, I know. But, I've got to try." In my mind, nothing was going to detour me. I just saw this as already happening and I would not let it go, cowering in some corner with a bunch of doubt. I had to try.

We drove in my car over to the venue and there was no place to park legally close to the back door which was in an alley. Regardless, I parked there, not caring if I was towed. We approached the back door and there were several people in front of us. Some went inside and some were turned away. Nervous hesitation of being turned away hit me, but now I was finally next in line at the door. The man answering the door was big and brawny. I told him that I had written Tom Petty a letter and wanted to see if I could get in. He was a huge man with dark hair and he gave me a crazy scowl. He said, "What's your name?" I told him my name and he looked at a clipboard he was holding. He asked me to verify that I was who I said I was and I showed him my ID. He said, "Follow me, Lyra. Mr. Petty wants to talk to you". He would not let my roadie friend come inside at all. It was February and cold. He had to stand in the alley and wait. I thought this was strange since he had been on the set up crew.

Once inside, my view was of a long line of at least a hundred people leaning against the wall waiting to shake Tom's hand. They stood along an extended hallway that seemed to slope down under the stadium. At first, I thought I would be just another one waiting in this endless line. That didn't happen though. I was escorted past all of them. Many of those waiting had a look on their face like "who is she?" I felt like I was being transported into a new world suddenly. The line seemed to be so long with people waiting to get a handshake or glimpse of the band. I was so glad that something different was happening and I was extremely nervous too. Then, we hit a set of doors.

The big guy escorting me knocked on the door and it was opened by another person I did not recognize. I was welcomed in and standing right there was Tom Petty waiting to talk to me. I was completely blown away. Mike Campbell sat on the couch over to the left. He smiled, spoke very little and was rather quiet. Tom and I stood together, our noses literally six inches apart. He was much more handsome in person, dressed casually of course. I remember thinking that his straight blonde hair looked so healthy, silky and it made you want to touch it. I was a little in shock and wondered how I could have thought about getting on stage with him at that point. My knees felt like rubber.

Tom told me that my letter had really touched him and he wanted to thank me and meet me in person. He said that due to rules they had to follow, it would not be possible for me to sing with him. However, he wanted me to send him a demo tape. He called behind him for someone and they appeared with a piece of paper with the address to send it to. We chatted awhile longer. Honestly I cannot even tell you what he said any further or what I replied with. I was just in such a nervous, excited state that I probably appeared like a bumbling idiot. I tried to be cool though. I think we talked about music mostly and I remember telling him I didn't have a demo tape but that I would have one made and promised to send it.

What struck me was how easy going he was -- just so humble and nice. He told me I was welcome to enjoy the show backstage and stay with others who would be there if I wanted to. I told him about my car being in the alley and that I had better get it moved. I thanked him profusely and said goodbye to Mike and Tom, making my way back up the long hallway toward the alley door.

I was not just smiling. I was radiant during this walk. I found my roadie friend and by this time I was so damn elated it was spilling out of me. He was excited saying, "I cannot believe it. I cannot believe this just happened for you. Do you know how big this is?" Yes, I did. He kept exclaiming his disbelief. I felt like I had been struck by a magic lightning bolt.

I found a phone booth and called my parents telling them where I was and that I had just met Tom Petty in person and he had invited me to stay backstage for the concert. My mom was insistent that she could not keep my daughter any longer and that I had to come and get her now. I pleaded with her. Finally, I asked her to put dad on the phone thinking he could convince her. I knew they didn't know who Tom Petty was or the significance, but it made no difference. They wanted me to come get their granddaughter right then and that is what I did.

I parted ways with my Alice Cooper Band friend and picked up my daughter. That was a major bummer, but I was so happy that I did get to meet the man in person and was treated so special. He treated me like I was the star. Truly, he was an incredible, humble person.

When we have such a burning intention to do something, a way can be made. It may not all happen exactly as we originally conceived it, but always intention fueled by desire drives the bus in our lives.

My roadie friend who showed up at the door at the right time to take the letter helped make it possible. He took my letter and somehow it did get to Tom. Intuitive urges prompted me to know when I should leave that bar and get over to the venue. Even the writing of the letter was another act of listening to my intuition. The scene at the bar where the roadie asks me what's in the letter produced a tiny moment of doubt as I knew he thought I was crazy. Yet, I denounced all doubt and ruled it by intention, putting the action behind it. I just wish I had kept my parents waiting a bit!

UFOs & A Little Help From My Friends

"What you seek is seeking you"
~ Jalaluddin Rumi

Despite the high and excitement from my Tom Petty meeting, normal life called. I continued with the office equipment sales, very much struggling to meet the high quota the company required in order to advance my salary each month. I was reaching the point where I either had to make that quota or quit. Otherwise, they would just fire me.

I was divorced and a single parent living in a rental condominium I could not really afford. While not fancy, it was in a better neighborhood than the previous one. The cover band that I fronted on most weekends helped to provide extra money. My child's father paid support, but it was not very much. I eventually left that job which I did not enjoy and took another legal secretarial position.

I began asking other musicians how I could get a good quality demo tape made and while it was not an exorbitant cost, it was more than I currently had together. I put the idea on the back burner for a few weeks.

On some Sundays, I would attend a spiritualistic or metaphysical church where I felt more comfortable being with people who shared my views. It was small and easy to know everyone due to its size. Sheila was a friend of mine from the church. One particular Sunday, I told her that I would be moving soon because I just couldn't afford where I was living. Unfortunately, I would have to move back into my parents' house which I did not want to do. Sheila suggested that I come and meet her roommates, adding that they had a large house with extra room for my child and me.

My daughter and I made a visit to check out this new possible situation and I knew from the outset that this would be very different for us. First, we would be living with two other women, one of whom had children, plus a man. Yet, it was more the way they lived. It was communal style, just not on a farm somewhere in the middle of nowhere.

I liked that there were other kids living there and my little girl would have children to play with. The large home had moderately high utilities and we would all chip in on the food cost. Basically, I had a certain amount to contribute each paycheck period toward rent, utilities and food. I would still just make it by the skin of my teeth.

The vibe there was very different and welcoming. My new roommates were very much into holistic ways of life and vocal about their spiritual beliefs and studies. This made life there pleasantly different. An eclectic guest list of visitors was a constant. We often had people coming over to meditate or just hang out for awhile. One man who was dating one of the other women spent some weekends there. He was very heavy into his meditation practice and it was not uncommon to walk into the dining room and find him on the floor in lotus position at different times of the day or night. I always felt bad intruding but he would open his eyes, greet me and smile as if no harm done.

A massage therapist made occasional visits and I was always intrigued with the small brown leather case of oils he carried, all with a different purpose. I wanted to learn about each of them and would ask so many questions. This small group I lived with seemed to have tentacle like arms that reached out and brought in all sorts of interesting individuals. While many of the things we were doing may not seem strange now, they were in the early 1980's, especially in the area of the United States I lived in.

One weekend night as I arrived home from a gig, my roommates greeted me at the door and they were full of excitement. They had flown with our friend and pilot, Don Elkins, and spent time with Uri Geller. Indeed, he had bent some spoons for them. They all seemed to gain a lot from their encounter with Uri and sharing their experiences with him as well. They talked about how they wish I had been on the trip, but I could not go due to work that night with the band.

This is the first place I ate seaweed soup. Talk about a tonic cleanser for your body! I spent most of the night in the bathroom. Sheila and I befriended a small group of Native Americans and would sit in circle with them, chanting and passing the peace pipe. These young people with strong Native American bloodlines also believed in the "star people".

The circle ritual would consist of a cleansing first with a bundle of sage or cedar that is lighted and passed around the circle. Each participant would hold the bundle and whirl the smoke around them. Sage was also used to remove negative thoughts and entities.

Next we would use a dried bundle of sweet grass to add positive vibes to the circle. Finally, I remember passing their peace pipe which would have real tobacco in it and sometimes other things such as marijuana. The circle ritual was performed in a relaxed way and they would teach us basic messages in their tribe that would be extended to the great beyond. These messages or chants were repeated in English which helped us remember what each prayer chant meant.

Everyone who lived in the house with me was at least ten years older, although I can't say I knew their exact ages. Another girl moved in who was just finishing up her chemical engineering degree. She was only slightly older than me. She and the male in the household soon became paramours.

One lively character we lived with was Jena. Sexually free, Jena was always talking about sex, making jokes about sex, telling stories of her escapades, and never shy about telling a guy she wanted to have sex. Some of this seemed to be to get a reaction and well, who knows? Jena was incredibly nice to everyone. She had a big heart and she was sexy in her own right for sure. While I had my own hang ups about things that probably made no sense, she was very free with her mental concepts of sexuality.

Sheila was more reserved, but I suspected a firestorm hid under her façade. She was my closest friend at the house and had two children, a boy and girl. Her children were as special and unique as she was and her daughter babysat for me years later as she grew into a teen. She had written an incredible fictional story for school that was so amazing and showed her natural gift for imaginative writing.

All of my friends were familiar with and a part of the world of metaphysics in various genres of study. The one paranormal area where they all had intense common interest was channeling sessions that were led by our friend, Carla Rueckert. Carla also worked in assisting others to channel as well. Carla did not live with us. She lived with Don Elkins and Jim McCarty and they held their own sessions at their home as well. We called our channeling sessions: UFO Meditation.

There was a book given to me when I moved into the house called *The Secrets of the UFOs*. Written and published by Don Elkins and Carla Rueckert, it contained information channeled prior to me joining the meditations. It also contained interviews or hypnosis sessions from persons who had experienced extraterrestrial contact of some sort. I suppose this is how our channeling sessions of the higher beings came to be known as UFO Meditation Group.

Before I disappoint, I want to come clean and let you know that I have never seen alien craft that I know of. I did have an incident around the age of sixteen. I was with a guy friend in a car and he had parked in a somewhat remote area. I was not interested in making out with him so the strange thing that happened next was a welcome diversion.

It was night and we sat there talking with the car engine shut off. Suddenly, we noticed a silent aerial vehicle hovering just above where we were parked. It stayed there for a long period of time. It did have lights and seemed dark in color, but with it being night, it was hard to tell what color it was. Giggling, we both joked of the alien possibility but we did not experience missing time or other anomalies that people report with abductions. Yet, the appearance of it did spook us a bit and we left with him driving me home.

My otherworldly or what some might call alien experience has all taken place on the level of the mind. I involved myself in meditating and channeling sessions of those existing in higher dimensions than we here on earth. I would not say that these entities are in outer space, but a higher place, unseen from this dimension with our human eyes. Some would call them extraterrestrials because they do not inhabit our planet. Yet, I see them as just beings from another dimension.

Sheila had been to Thailand and other areas of the planet learning the major spiritual tenant of eastern religions. She had experimented with many things, occasionally finding nirvana and sometimes very trying situations. She would share interesting stories with me including being held in a Thai prison for awhile. Jena and Sheila had hung out with people like Ram Dass and were true children of the sixties.

Located in an older working class neighborhood, the house we inhabited was a large white two story with siding. There were steps in the front leading to a fairly large front porch with a swing. As you entered the front door, a parlor type room to the right served as the place where we held channeling sessions and it was pretty much dedicated to that purpose. We found it more conducive to keep the energy in that room just for that special purpose, although I am sure this rule was broken at times.

These were people that truly tried to live their spiritual path daily and were quite dedicated to it. I was twenty-three and although very much on a spiritual quest, could not say I was grounded in a spiritual discipline of any sort. I was learning constantly and experimenting, dipping my toe in the water to check the temperature before diving in.

I had a deep interest in metaphysics that had progressed from my teen years. By twenty-two, I had taught myself to mathematically calculate natal and transiting western astrological charts for myself and friends. Computers were non-existent so this was all done with an ephemeris and hand drawn charts. This was despite the fact that I did not excel in mathematics. I felt I had done this charting before and have become convinced I may have in an earlier life as it came so natural to me. Interpretation of the charts was more complicated and it would take years to get better at that.

Though I had certain psychic abilities, I was reluctant to delve deeply with them. It was as if there was an invisible fence line that I would come up against within my studies and I would say, "Whoa, I'm not going over this fence into the next yard because I don't know what is there." This fear continued for years in one way or another. Cautiously, I would hurdle one fence, only to find myself encountering another new one and putting the brakes on myself again. I attributed much of this to fears I had picked up along the way from the Baptist church I had attended.

I was intensely interested in the subject of consciousness in general and in as much detail as was available at the time. For me, science had not made the strides I would later learn of. Therefore, most of what I learned about consciousness was from spiritual studies alone.

Often, my roommates and I spoke of personal responsibility and free will, knowing that both were tied together in a package that had to be assimilated to progress further. Sheila and Jena often proclaimed that we had all chosen to be here together and that we were all "one".

The only introduction I had to channeling was a book *"The God of Jane"* by Jane Roberts, which I had read some months before meeting Sheila. This was a compilation and story of how Jane Roberts came to channel the entity known as Seth. It was not coincidental that I had purchased and read that book a few months earlier. It was an off-topic book for me to be interested in. Reflecting now, I see it as just another synchronicity to ready me for actual channeling with my friends.

Our UFO meditation groups were a bit different but the principle was the same. We were channeling a group consciousness or beings from another dimension. These beings had already experienced similar life existences in the third density we inhabit. They had graduated at various points to where they were now, namely fourth, fifth and sixth densities. What we had in common with these entities is that we were all striving to raise our vibration or consciousness to grow closer to the one true God Source. Part of being able to do that was providing service to this planet through imparting this knowledge which could be used or discarded as the receiver saw fit. The channeled group entities were serving in their own way and we would hopefully serve in our own individual ways. The emphasis was in service to others rather than service to self.

For me, hanging with my roommates made me grow quickly in the light and love of the one true infinite Creator God Source. It was as if I picked up knowledge through osmosis from just being around them. I often expressed that I was not as good, behind in my progress and felt inferior in some way. They were all so loving – hugging me and telling me that I was an adept, just remembering who I really was. We would all laugh and hug, but I didn't really believe it.

In my mind, I had too many faults and not enough experience to be adept at anything. I had this wild self confidence that allowed me to front a band, but inside I felt not good enough and smaller than everyone around me. I had a very hard time expressing my needs, asking and receiving.

Carla was channeling fourth and fifth density beings during our circle meditations held on weekends. Privately at home, she was channeling a sixth density group of entities called Ra with Jim and

Don. She was doing this in a trance state instead of our usual sitting upright on couches and chairs meditative state. Trance is a much deeper brainwave level state in which Carla appeared to be asleep and allowing the group entity known as "Ra" to speak through her.

During these three person, private trance sessions, Carla would lie down, an altar placed above her head with the Holy Bible open to the Gospel of John. Included also was a candle, incense and other little things that were significant to her. She was creating a safe, loving atmosphere for herself, Jim and Don to allow this sixth density entity to come through her while she was completely out of normal conscious awareness. Due to the higher vibration of this sixth density group consciousness, the trance state appeared to be the best way for contact and it also was able to come through with these three individuals as participants due to their energy or resonance they held as a cohesive unit.

Collectively, the channeling of both groups gave a history of planetary and galactic evolution to date along with principles for living now and being able to move or "graduate" to the next higher density. This involved the concept of service to others over service to self. It was not a religion, but more a philosophy. To some, it could be looked at as secret tips to make sure you don't get stuck having to reincarnate and learn the same lessons over again. This puts it all in simplified terms for this memoir. Yet, the information is vast and goes deep into many aspects of the purpose of being and life.

My thoughts jumped up and down, for and against the channeling while I lived there. At times, I was afraid of what we could be bringing in. I did express these fears to my roommates who would affirm that this is possible and reiterate to me that as long as we are coming from a very high vibration state and protecting ourselves psychically, all would be well. They also were always quick to let me know that all negative entities can be dispelled by sending them love and light.

The philosophy and practice of living in love and light was active in our home. The house, itself, had a very loving feel upon entering. There was not only the laughter of adults and children, but there was a peace that comes from treating each other with loving respect.

Ashamedly, I betrayed our trust together while living there. We each had a debit card for the general bank account that we put our funds into for bill paying, food, etc. One day, I needed money for something. I do not even recall what, but I made an ATM withdraw without telling my roommates about it. This, of course, messed up the balance they expected to be there. I intended to pay it back and it was not a great amount of money, less than forty dollars. However, I was not forthcoming and up front about it. I did not know why. My thinking was that I would deposit that money back into the account when I was paid along with what I would normally put in.

I was not trying to be purposely deceptive with them but I am sure it appeared that way. On some level, I did not want them to think I needed anything. Isn't this crazy? We all need things. Why could I have not worked something out, letting them know up front before I made the withdraw?

When it was found out, they all confronted me. I offered my jigsaw puzzle explanation which made no sense to me at the time and they instantly forgave me. This made me feel even worse. It was not a truthful act, but they forgave me and I really did not know how to process that kind of reaction. I had not forgiven myself and this added more to my sense of not good enough. The reaction I would have received from my own family would have been so dramatically different than the love and forgiveness felt from these people.

One weekend, Sheila invited me to go along with her for a reading by a lady she said was very good at psychic tarot cards. I had been to a couple of these readers in the past with another friend and was game for it. We arrived at the medium's small country home which was filled with numerous figurines of things she felt close to – her totems. It was a conglomeration of American Indian, fairy and religious figures. It made her entire living room décor seem more like a gift shop, but I was not judging.

Following the lady toward the back of her house, I began my reading with her first. The clairvoyant seemed to connect with my maternal grandfather. She also asked me who was crazy about apple juice. My daughter was going through a phase where she wanted to drink a lot of the juice and the tarot card reader said spirit was saying to let her have all she wanted. She told me that I was someone who had fallen victim to the guise of love in the past.

She was using a Rider/Waite deck. Based on two cards, the Knight of Swords and the Knight of Cups, she told me that I had two loves coming in my life. One would be dark and very irresistible to me for some reason. She warned that he was not the one and I would experience much undue strife with that relationship. She stated the other one I would meet may not have the same intense charisma, but was much lighter in spirit and would truly love me. Warnings I failed to listen to would unfold in my future.

There was a small neighborhood bar and restaurant that Sheila and I had been to a couple of times. She invited me to come along with her one evening and we were having a great time enjoying different local acoustic acts. With it being Sunday, the place closed at 12:30 a.m. We were invited to go to a party at one of the owner's homes. Sheila indicated it was cool and I could see that she liked this owner for more than just a friend.

Once at the party, all the guitars started coming out. Everyone was playing and singing. I performed a cover of *Landslide* by Fleetwood Mac and my voice was particularly resonant and rich that evening. The acoustics were great inside, even though it seemed like a regular living room. Amidst the party chatter, the circle of guitars began playing and I began singing. The entire room became very quiet. It was either real good or real bad. The crowd indicated it was incredibly good.

After I sang, a few girls came up to me and told me they were getting ready to start an all girl band. They wanted me to be in it. I told them I already had a band, but I was okay with checking it out and I really appreciated them asking me.

Tall, dark and handsome approached me for conversation. His hair was thick, almost jet black. His eyes were hazel sometimes looking green, at other times brown. He was also a musician. He and I hit it off immediately in the physical attraction department, but I did notice something right away that I should have taken to heart. He said, "Wow, you really sounded incredible, but did you notice you were singing just a tiny bit under the note". He then went into a diatribe about perfect pitch and how almost no one has it. I didn't really take offense to his comment because I knew he liked my singing and I also knew others did as well. It rolled right past me. I should have taken it as a major clue to his critical nature, but I did not want to be seen as someone who could not take any form of constructive criticism.

We began seeing each other and I discovered what a rebel at life he was. I fell for him, however, big time. Isn't that what young, stupid girls do --- go for the mysterious, can't corral cowboy? Sheila warned me that she felt he was too "dark" for me. The psychic tarot reader did as well. I didn't listen.

He did not believe in our channeling sessions and thought it was all fake and ridiculous. He had never attended a session or read any of the literature. Like many, he thought that channeling was bunk. I admit it is a crazy concept when you try to explain it to someone.

We had a tumultuous relationship for years – about eleven years. The channeled material by Carla and company catches up with me again thirty years later – by more synchronicities.

Miracle

> "Rock bottom became the solid foundation
> on which I rebuilt my life."
> ~ J.K. Rowling *(Harvard Speech)*

As dark as Sheila believed Nathan to be, I could not see it. I only saw the light in him and the goodness – because good and bad exists in everyone. Sheila gently counseled me when I asked her opinion of him, but she was not about to infringe upon my free will. I chose to keep seeing him.

When we engage in a close relationship with someone, we see a mirror of our own qualities at first, especially during the falling in love or infatuation stage. As time goes on, the other person can begin to reflect things that exist within our own shadow self that we are challenged to see clearly, confront and transform.

Nathan was spotty with his work habits. He sometimes did construction work and at times would perform solo gigs playing acoustically in various bars. He sang like a songbird being gifted with a beautiful manly voice. He used that voice and his guitar to sway me and other ladies easily. When he wanted to turn on the charm, he certainly could. Often his song choices were quite romantic.

He knew I had met Tom Petty and that I wanted to make a demo tape. I had a plan of going to Nashville and make a good quality tape in a studio there. He always told me that I was not really that good; that my band performed the most stupid, popular music instead of the really cool artistic stuff. I idolized Nathan and his talent. I felt maybe he knew more than I. Yet, I was the one that had a working band. He was lucky to play a very small venue once or twice a month. Most of the time, he played for free with friends at after hours parties that would crop up at various musicians' homes.

As time passed, I allowed him to slowly chisel away at my self confidence with his put-downs. I eventually quit my band, stating artistic differences when I wanted to perform some of the music Nathan had suggested.

This was sad that I let him put me and the music we performed down as if it and I were not good enough. The fact is, I had been having fun with those sets of songs and feeling great excitement about the entire experience with my band mates and our audiences. After dating Nathan, I found myself worrying about each song in every set. Did it reflect artistically the way it should? In other words, did it meet the critical demands of Nathan?

Inside, I will always be the girl who broke her promise to herself and Tom Petty. I never made or sent the demo tape. I will die being the girl that did not take her dream further because I let the illusion of love and my intense need to be loved detour my plans. I allowed someone else to play that familiar game with me, telling me in one way or another: you're not good enough. My life could have taken an entirely different path.

It is a shame I did not follow through and chase my dream further. With the demo tape never made, I would always have that question about how things could have gone. Failure was a distinct possibility. Tom Petty may have never phoned and said a word to me about the tape. Then again, who knows? I learned later in life that you don't have to be the best in the music business to have a thriving career. Sometimes, it is who you know and the opportunities that open up for you. To this day, I have that piece of paper from Tom Petty.

Nathan was also manic depressive. He was the epitome of a frustrated artistic type who cannot get their act together. The codependent in me wanted to help save him from his inner monsters. Eventually, his monsters started striking out at me. It was in small ways at first and they increased over time.

He drank almost every night and I found myself hanging in bars with him until the wee hours on some weekend nights, only to go back to his place and either have sex or a fight. Nathan knew exactly what to do at a very core level to agitate someone to the point of anger. He was very smart, zeroing in on any weakness you had and making a strike as quickly as a snake would bite. Once he had driven me to reacting verbally, Nathan would snicker or laugh with delight that he had thrown me off balance emotionally. This was just a control technique, but I could not see it clearly for what it was. It escalated later as he became more abusive.

It is a mistake to always believe that if I guy takes you to meet his family that he is serious about you. Looking back, I think Nathan took me to meet his mom because he didn't have any money to take me out. Eating dinner at his mom's house was an easy date for him. In my mind, I thought our first few months of being together were now something more serious.

Yet meeting his mom was a good thing for me and it began another series of synchronicities. Beginning the trip there in my car, I inquired where his mom lived. He said "Hemlock Hill Apartments". "Oh, I used to live there. It's a nice complex" I said. However, when we arrived at the apartment complex and parked the car, we went to the same building I had lived in. He subsequently knocked on the door of the very same apartment I had lived in. It was uncanny.

When I inhabited what was now his mother's apartment, a couple lived across the hall. The husband played banjo and I would often hear him practicing. Nathan now owned that banjo, having bought it from the couple prior to his mother moving to the apartment complex. He could have purchased it when I lived there but he was unsure of the exact year he had bought it.

Nathan's parents were divorced and I did not meet his father for awhile. However, I discovered from talking to my dad that Nathan's father had been his Boy Scout Eagle instructor and occasional math tutor. Additionally, Nathan's father and mother were dating at the time of my own father's relationship with Nathan's dad. They had jointly arranged for the Eagle Scouts to go on their first date which was chaperoned by Nathan's parents as one large group date, an outdoor picnic event of some sort.

So, all of these incredible synchronicities were occurring in a metropolitan area of approximately 800,000 to one million people. And with multitudes of apartment complexes in all areas of the city, I found myself looking at these coincidences and thinking it meant that he and I were star-crossed and meant to be together.

Still to this day, I believe Nathan was meant to be a part of my life and story. At times, I see the meaning behind our relationship and how we both fell into something that reflected what each of us needed to address. We actually were star-crossed. This does not mean it was to be the best relationship of my life, but one in which he served as a tremendous catalyst to eventually catapult me in other directions.

I allowed Nathan to slowly eat away at my "twenty something" self-esteem and who I was. He would often tell me in no uncertain terms that I was "over confident" and not capable of all I thought I was. I did ignore this, but slowly, over time, and with enough of his constant critical statements, I began to believe this as well. It was especially at low moments that this was easy to happen. He did not even need to be around me. His words would echo in my mind when I was having a down time.

As time progressed, Nathan yelled the most cutting remarks at me during arguments. He knew about the child I had given up for adoption and would often tell me that no one else would want me since I had children by three different men. He said I was fat and I may have only been ten pounds overweight. He often said I was book smart with no common sense. He would even tell me that my head was strangely shaped. Even if it were, what could anyone do about that? All the comments were meant to beat me down and keep me in my place in the relationship. I just could not see it. I held a place deep inside me that did believe I was flawed. I couldn't see my gifts and goodness clearly all the time. At low moments, his words held such weight with me sinking me further into my corrupted beliefs.

About two years into my relationship with Nathan, I began having sporadic episodes of vaginal bleeding that did not coincide on a rhythmic basis with my period. I believed I had cancer and started calling doctors in the yellow pages to get an appointment to be seen. Everyone that I called had a long wait time of many weeks. I made an appointment with the doctor who had the shortest wait time of 3 weeks.

I was unemployed at this time and living with Nathan at his house along with my daughter. Nathan did not have to work as hard as most. His house was run down, but it was free. It had been given to him by his father. Ugly and in need of repair, the bare wood flooring in the bathroom was falling through in places. He seemed disinterested in actually fixing anything, talking about it only from time to time. He had very low motivation and no follow through.

My vaginal bleeding became worse and it was always bright red. I finally went to the emergency room, dropping my daughter off with a friend so I could get some answers. There was not a long wait, but the results that came back were shocking. No, it was not cancer. I was pregnant.

They wanted to perform an ultrasound to look at the fetus. The ultrasound showed that the placenta was lodged close to the cervix area, instead of to the side or an upper area. This meant that as the baby grew, it was putting pressure on the placenta and this was causing the bleeding. I was also about fifteen or sixteen weeks along in the pregnancy. I just did not know with the constant bleeding.

I had noticed my stomach expanding some, but felt it was some sort of bloating that was occurring from my unknown gynecological problem. The thought of pregnancy had entered my mind a couple of times, but I believed it impossible with the bleeding.

I went back and told Nathan and he was enraged over it saying he was not going to have any kids, telling me I would have to get an abortion. I told him I didn't have the money for an abortion if I wanted to have one and besides, this baby was too far along. He allowed me to stay at his house awhile longer while I tried to save money to get out on my own. Honestly, there was a part of me that wanted him to be happy about the baby. I kept thinking he might change his mind, just like I kept thinking I might change him. He didn't change his mind. I obtained another legal secretarial job and kept trying to get money together as quick as paychecks would occur.

Even though I knew this was a very high risk pregnancy with the placenta problem, I began feeling excited about the baby. I had already been told by the physician team I was seeing at the hospital that the delivery would have to be by cesarean section. The placenta which is feeding oxygen to the baby cannot be vaginally delivered prior to the baby. The baby would die and I might as well.

My tummy grew quickly now and I had to purchase some maternity clothes for work. It could not be some big t-shirt. I had to look professional and nice. At a second hand store, I found three different outfits that I would alternate. I bought one nice looking dress from a department store that was marked down. It had not been easy to tell my ultra conservative bosses that I was pregnant and yes, not married.

At night, Nathan would leave and go make his rounds at bars. Once I got my daughter down to sleep, I would cry. I found myself hopelessly wishing Nathan would change. I vacillated between that and wanting to buy some item for the baby. I spent a few dollars of my paycheck on a baby blanket and a couple of other items. Nathan saw them and it tripped his brain. Angry as ever, he told me I had two days to move out. He said if I had the money to buy baby items, I had the money to move out. Snow was accumulating outside. It was a very cold January. I knew he meant business. He was so enraged and perhaps on the verge of violence.

I immediately started calling apartment ads and looking around. I found a place on the lower east side of town. I had managed to save some money and called my father and told him what was going on. I dreaded telling my parents this. Pregnant again, what in the world would they think? I impressed upon my dad that I had found a place to rent and had put down the deposit and first month's rent. I told him "Dad, he wants me out now."

God bless my father and uncle. They both came with pickup trucks and moved what large items I had with the snow on the ground and more on the way. My own bed was actually at my parent's house and that would have to be brought in a day or so separately.

But I had the keys to my new place and it would be great for my little girl and the baby on the way. It was one-half of a house, a duplex basically. The neighborhood was not too far from Nathan's mom. Everything was on the first floor except my daughter's room. She had a huge attic bedroom and separate playroom for all her toys.

The day's move had worn me out completely, not to mention the psychological aspects of it all. I really felt it was over. I was now on my own with this. Nathan would not be any help or care about his child. His selfishness completely astounded me, but I had bigger things to think about. I only had forty dollars left until my next paycheck. I needed groceries, enough gasoline to get to work, and a stove. I only had a refrigerator.

I slept on the floor that night because my bed had not yet been moved to the duplex. My pregnant body ached so intensely from the items I had packed in my car and moved by myself in the snow. The pain, combined with thoughts of how much money I had left until my next paycheck, haunted me. Sleep was not forthcoming even though I was exhausted. I had enough money to buy a used stove or get groceries for myself and my daughter, but not both. I had no way to cook anything and I was so tired and confused. I wasn't thinking out of the box. Looking back, I may have been able to go to a second hand store and pick up a crock pot or hot plate. However, my mind was jumbled and worried. I just prayed. I prayed over and over again asking God for help with the stove and food situation. I fell asleep on the floor, crying and asking for help.

In the morning, my daughter woke and we had cereal together while sitting at the table beside the kitchen window. My eyes were red and puffy from the night before. My pregnant belly felt a little better from the rest. The snow was now more than a foot on the ground and my daughter was, of course, excited to play in it.

The duplex apartment sat on the corner of a small side street of mostly single family homes. I watched as two men emerged from the house across the side street. One propped the side door of the house open and they both went inside. I wondered why they would have the door open because it was bitterly cold. Suddenly, they both began carrying an old stove outside and placing it on the porch. Bingo! The bell struck in my head and I told my daughter to stay put while I grabbed my snow boots and coat. I made my way outside quickly because I did not want to miss them as they moved back inside.

I yelled, "Hi, I'm your new neighbor. What are you doing with that stove? Are you getting rid of it?" The homeowner made his way over through the thick snow and said that his wife had a new stove and the old one was just taking up room. I told him I didn't have the money for it now, but I would be happy to pay him later for it as long as it works. "Oh, it works", he said. "She just wanted something newer, updating the kitchen." There was a slight pause as he looked at my now protruding stomach from my coat. "I would love to have it. How much money do you want for it?" I asked. He said "Well, my buddy and I will bring it over here." And they did. I had a stove and he insisted on giving it to me for free. I could not thank him enough and I felt somewhat indigent with the situation but I could not focus on a silly thing like pride. My prayer had been so instantly answered!

I would now have groceries until my next pay period. I was going to make it. I literally praised and thanked God all that day and for several days for what I considered to be a timely miracle. I truly felt touched by divine synchronicity and God's grace. This made such an impact on me. It literally turned my attitude toward one of hope instead of despair.

As much as I needed this item, the neighbor needed a way to rid his household of an old, but working stove. We both had components that led to what some would call coincidence. Yet, it is the timing of the event and the outdoor weather conditions that could lead anyone to see this as miraculous. He may have been thinking what am I going to do with this old stove? He may have worried that he did not want it sitting on the side porch for a long time. We were both solutions for each other and his generosity in bringing the stove through all that snow, hooking it up and making it free for me was further proof of the synchronicity. He could have thought to charge me something had he a different attitude.

As my baby grew, the bleeding episodes continued and one in particular was quite serious. I was admitted to the hospital for two days and then ordered to be on bed rest the entire rest of the pregnancy. I was given drugs to keep me from going into labor prematurely but it was critical that I did not do a lot of walking around.

I had to leave my job and I only had a small amount of child support coming in each month for my first daughter – two hundred dollars to be exact. That was not going to cover the bills each month. I lived super simply going without many things like a home telephone. Remember, cell phones were not in existence at this time. My main bills were electric, gas and rent for the duplex.

Hesitant to ask my parents for help, I was behind on things and always trying to play catch up financially. My mother was completely irate with me about the pregnancy. Upon a visit to my parents' home, she had actually kicked me in the rear end while pregnant. I do not remember her hurtful words, but she actually kicked me as I was leaving her house. I did not see her again for quite some time. While I was not injured, who kicks people – much less a pregnant woman?

Nathan's mom knew of the pregnancy. Unlike Nathan, she was very excited about being a grandmother. She helped me tremendously. I also received some sick pay from my job which I had to just leave suddenly. I managed to qualify for food stamps.

In the middle of the night in March, I began bleeding and it would not stop. I sat over the toilet and yelled for my seven year old daughter until she awoke. We had an arrangement that if I had a medical emergency, she could use the telephone of the neighbor in the adjoining duplex unit. To say that it was raining that night would be an understatement. It was pouring down buckets. My daughter put on her coat, grabbed an umbrella making her way over to the neighbor's. She asked them to call an ambulance and Nathan's mother. She took care of both in a very grown up way at only seven years old. Standing outside in the pouring rain with the umbrella, my daughter waited to waive down the ambulance.

Once they arrived, I had lost a lot of blood. They immediately packed me into the ambulance and I felt very weak. I could hear them calling my vital signs into the hospital emergency room. I don't remember the exact numbers, but my blood pressure was extremely low.

The trip was bumpy, but quick. They wheeled me into the emergency room, then straight to surgery. I knew my blood type, but they had to type me quickly anyway, just as protocol. The anesthesiologist was standing at my head getting ready to put a mask on my mouth. I made eye contact and asked him to please take good care of me. In my mind, the vitals – the blood loss was so significant – I thought the baby was probably in jeopardy. I was also six weeks early for this delivery. With the pressure of the growing baby pushing against the placenta, my body just could not hold out any longer. It seemed the baby's birth time had arrived.

When I woke from the general anesthesia, my vision was limited and very blurry, but I could hear. I began crying and the doctor told me all was fine and that my baby had a bit of trouble breathing at first but was doing great now. "She was just big enough to breathe on her own" he said. I was relieved to hear this. I asked him, "how much, how much?" He said, "Don't worry about the bill right now." "No" I said, "How much did she weigh?" "Five pounds fourteen ounces" Wow, she was tiny. Okay, but she was breathing on her own I thought. He then mentioned that she had the most hair he had ever seen on a baby and he laughed.

I didn't feel any pain as I gradually came to. They wheeled me to a room and I stayed put in my bed. I had no choice after the surgery. Shortly thereafter, Nathan's mom came in and she was so excited. The baby was in intensive care, mostly just for monitoring. She said, "There is nothing wrong with that baby girl. When I saw her, she was stretching her legs up in the air and very active." Still, I wanted to see her for myself.

I told the next nurse that came into my room, "I have to see my baby. Can I go see her?" She told me I probably needed to stay put for a few more hours. "You've lost a lot of blood and with the c-section, tomorrow would probably be the time we want to get you up and moving just a bit." I begged her. About an hour later, she brought a wheelchair. I felt like I was pushing heavy blocks of lead to move myself into a sitting position with my legs on the side of the bed. They then assisted me into the wheelchair. It was painful, but I didn't care. I had to see my baby and she was everything Nathan's mother said and more. Within a day, she was moved out of intensive care and I was able to feed her.

Informed of the birth, Nathan showed up at the hospital but expressed a ridiculous amount of fear about coming and that he was not to be identified as the father of the baby. He was so afraid of having to pay child support. Still, I romanticized the event in my mind, thinking that once he saw his baby girl he would 'change'. To an extent, he did. He acted out his controlling possessiveness about the baby and me. I took this to mean 'love'. It was not real love. I could have seized this time we had not been seeing each other to rid him permanently from my life, but I didn't. I kept wishing and hoping he would change.

He still did not contribute financially to me when I was obviously in need of help. Instead, he would stay now at my apartment sometimes. Other times, he would be off doing his nightly bar visits. He tried to cut me off from other family members discouraging me from seeing them. Nathan did all this to remain in control of a situation he was not man enough to be truly responsible toward.

Nathan's mom took care of so many things for me. She cleaned up all the blood at my apartment which she half-jokingly said looked like Charles Manson had been there. She was a great friend to me and a wonderful grandmother to my daughter.

My baby had no crib. I kept her in bed with me or a laundry basket with a blanket for a soft mattress at first. Within a couple of weeks, one of the girls from my old job came to see the baby and brought me a used bassinet. She was so tiny, this would do for awhile. Later, her grandmother bought her a baby bed. She would often bring me diapers and extra food.

Within eight weeks of my daughter's birth, the landlords informed me they were putting the duplex up for sale. I then had occasional showings by the owner or their real estate agent. Someone did purchase the property fairly quickly and I had to move.

In the meantime, I had managed to obtain some partial assistance with the cost of daycare through a community agency. I found a job for another attorney and began working again. It was a small single attorney practice and they knew I was a single mom, still nursing my new baby. I would pump at lunch and put the liquid into bottles, placing them in their refrigerator. Some days, if I had time, I would run over to my baby's daycare and feed her there. It was an expensive, but great, daycare owned by a nurse. Since I had returned to work when she was only four weeks old and six is the standard, I felt comfortable paying more for the better care. I hated going back to work so soon, but I had to with our financial situation so grim.

The attorney I worked for owned a few rental properties and had a vacancy at one of the apartments. He gave me the address and told me to go look at it since he knew I had to move soon. It had been completely renovated and was on the second floor of a Victorian home in an older section of town. I loved it. The bath was fresh with new tub, flooring, sink and toilet. The kitchen had also been renovated with new stove, countertops and refrigerator. New carpet and paint was throughout the living room and bedrooms. My rent would be the same amount per month as I was paying now. I made arrangements to make the move.

Nathan had become on again/off again with me – sometimes acting like a committed father and partner, most of the time not. My life was stressful and he actually was a huge part of that mixture. Finances can be a heavy strain on any single parent and I was exhausting everything I had within me to get better jobs that paid more money and advance my situation.

With two children now, I became more serious than ever about being responsible and trying to go farther in life. I applied for a job as a marketing coordinator at a local company and got the job. I reported directly to the President and Senior Vice President. Basically, this was a glorified title for an executive secretarial position.

Now, working for executives of a company, my job was very serious to me. I had to leave for the day with my "A" game on, after which I would go around picking up my girls in two different locations. Often, I would come home to find Nathan just waking up in my apartment at 6:00 pm. If I became upset about this, he told me I was "crazy" and that I just did not understand the schedules of night people. That may have been true if he was a person with a night job where he actually made money. I did not understand how he had the nerve to sleep in my bed all day while I got my little girls off to where they would go to school or stay until I could pick them up. I was working hard to be a good mommy to them, fix dinner, clean everything, and get up, go to work and do it all over again. That's what I did not understand.

One evening after work, I walked the steps up to my apartment with my baby and daughter, opened the door, found he had just arisen from bed. I didn't say a word to him. I went to the kitchen around the corner and opened the refrigerator to find he had eaten quite a bit of cheese and did not even bother to wrap it back up. He contributed nothing - not groceries, money, and he was continually eating my food, staying often at my apartment. I went crazy. I picked up a butcher knife, yelling at him about the cheese, purposely attacking and stabbing a wooden chair instead of him. He got his ass out of there quick. Okay, now you have proof that I am crazy, I thought. After that incident, he stayed away for awhile and I am sure used that time to go around telling everyone how 'crazy' I was.

Fall arrived and my oldest daughter had her 8th birthday. We celebrated at my apartment and many family members attended. My grandfather said, "Hey Lyra, did you know this was Katherine's house?" "Really?" I said. "Who is Katherine?" Katherine turned out to be a great aunt who was now deceased. I knew I felt a peace there and like it was a welcoming new start. I was meant to be living there for awhile. So, this was the second time I had a coincidence happen with where I had lived.

Yet change is always occurring around us. It is inevitable and the rental property was eventually sold. The new landlord was okay with me staying there at the same rate and I did. Eventually, my parents decided to purchase a second home for investment purposes – a small house in a neighborhood that my two girls and I could rent from them. We did just that and it remained our home from 1986 to 1994.

My relationship with my parents had certainly been strained over these years. However, they could see I was struggling to make it the best I could and wanted to help. It was very fortunate for us to have something that felt like a real home.

With the fresh start at the new neighborhood home, I told myself I would keep Nathan out of our lives. I can't remember what brought us together again, but I relented once more. While he did not live with me, he did stay with us often. He still paid no child support. Occasionally, he would fix something for me on my car or at the house. When he performed these tasks, it was like he had climbed Mount Everest and I should let him stay there for free - forever. In his mind, he had earned his rent and board.

Nathan was controlling and I would mistake this for caring about me. The only thing he really cared about was his immediate needs or comfort. Why was I doing this? Why did I think I was so in love with someone who did not know what love really was between a man and a woman?

Shame keeps us locked in our old stories and patterns. Subconsciously, we are telling ourselves that we are an action or idea of the past. We are only that if we continue those beliefs which, in turn, attract people and situations to us that reflect those ideas we are holding. I was confused about what real love looked like. Additionally, that feeling of not good enough was so deeply ingrained.

The synchronicity is just stacked in this time period. First, I encountered two places of living – one with Nathan's mother living in the same apartment I used to live in. In a city of many apartment complexes and in a complex that had hundreds of units – Nathan's mother lived in the exact apartment I used to live in. Nathan purchased his banjo from my neighbors across the hall prior to his mother moving there. I end up living in the second story of my deceased great aunt's former home.

My divine intervention was the gift of the stove. In desperation, I prayed and gave it up to God about the money situation and needing a solution – food or stove? The next morning, I had a stove and that left enough money for food.

I discovered that my father was mentored as a teen by my new baby's grandfather in Eagle Scouts and tutored with mathematics in a city of so many people. It was amazing they had shared this close relationship. Had he only known what would happen years into the future.

Overall, I fell to a place where I needed a tribe to help me. This came in the form of individuals who felt ready to give and grace that befell me. I also needed to help myself and become self sufficient. If not for the assistance of others at the time I really needed it, I would have fallen into nothing. Never give up on anyone and if you see them really trying to get it together, give a little more to them if you can.

I kept improving my work skills learning everything I could so that I could stay at that job for awhile, then apply for a better job within the company or somewhere else. I viewed everything in life as stepping stones and truly, I had fallen down to the bottom and was climbing the best I could each day.

Often, we don't want to look at what is not healthy for us. Underneath, burning at the bottom of us like a smoldering bed of coals that never dies, we develop some sort of outward problem that is merely a manifestation of avoidance. For some, this could be an addiction to alcohol or drugs. Other people develop food addictions, either refusal of food or eating too much of it. Certainly, there are kaleidoscopes of addictive behaviors that can be possible sources of avoiding what is really eating at you inside.

Mine was staying super busy and often working two jobs. Every single mother I know is going to be busier than most parents because they are trying to fill a position that ideally would be shared by two. Yet, I can see how I kept my mind and body constantly engaged in work and things to do at home with my girls to avoid thinking about what was really bothering me.

Part of this was my desire to get ahead financially as much as possible. Another part of it was avoidance. Yet, life has a way of constantly only attracting to us what we need to see and it usually comes in the form of those around us. Toxic relationships show us either the parts of ourselves we deny and do not want to own up to, or they show us how we experience self-love deprivation.

The Voice

"Give not that which is holy unto the dogs, neither cast ye your pearls before swine, lest they trample them under their feet, and turn again and rend you."

~ Matthew 7:6, The Holy Bible, King James Version

My on again-off again relationship with Nathan continued for years. When I would break up with him, he would show up at my house in the middle of the night, knocking on the windows and doors, often waking my little girls. Once, he kicked in the side door and his mother paid a carpenter to replace all the damage. He was wild and unpredictable. He would use our daughter as an excuse to get back in. Most of the time he was very charming and apologetic, phoning me saying he had changed. Nathan was incredibly smart and manipulative. He was a full blown mental case with personality disorders. Yet, he had me convinced that I was the one who was messed up. And I was, just in a different way.

He often threatened that calling the police would do no good when he was being abusive or broke into my house. He would proudly announce that by the time they got there, he would be gone. He made me feel powerless or I allowed him to, but I was so used to being stomped down by him that I couldn't see a way around it.

He was hypercritical of me and often told me that I was going to end up a lonely old woman with no one. This really disturbed me. He would point out character flaws and say, "See, this is why you are going to end up an old lonely woman." He would also try and make me feel that no one would ever want me. "Look at you!" he would say. "You've had three kids by three different men. No one is going to want you." I took it to heart, even though a part of me tried to resist this as being true. It was his truth yet I internalized it deeply.

I lived in hope that he would change, but it never happened. We must take people where they are and not where we know they could be. It is easy to see the goodness in someone and believe they can drop all that negative stuff and be the great, lighter parts. This so rarely happens. If you find yourself in a relationship where you want someone to "change", an alarm bell should be going off for you.

Regret that I stayed so long in the relationship has been present for me many times. It was like constantly trying to fit a square inside a circle and the geometry was just not going to work. I had also dreamed one night that Nathan was with another woman. That would not be the first time it had happened, but he was supposedly "changing" again.

When the dream ended, I awoke and drove to his house in the early morning hours. Just like in the dream, I turned the lock with my key to his front door, I walked to the bedroom, finding him with that woman passed out and naked in his bed. Abruptly I turned around, slamming the front door as I left. I broke off with him immediately, but he kept with his words of how sorry he was and he was just "drunk"; she didn't mean anything. For a few weeks, I did not listen to any of it and kept my distance from him. This time, I threatened him that I would call the police if he came near my house.

Yet, I allowed my loneliness and my illogical hope for him changing to bring us together once more. He would be extra nice during these reunion times and very romantic. Nathan knew what he was doing with his manipulative tactics. Dumb me believed he was really changing and actually felt sorry for him.

Over time, he became more violent and this seemed to coincide with me not reacting to his crude comments and horrible, negative nature. If I remained happy, my good mood provoked him to violence. Pinning me up against the wall, choking me until I thought I might die, I later told him when I could speak again, "you can kill me, but you can't take my soul." He glared at me with a strange dark look and stormed out of my house.

I loved weekend mornings when I did not have to rush out of the house getting my children to daycare and school. I could leisurely wake up and have a few minutes to think stress-free. As I lay in bed one particular morning with the sunlight streaming into the window, I heard a man's loud voice. He said, "Quit throwing your pearls to swine!" Startled, I jumped looking toward the corner of the room. The voice was just the same as if someone were standing right there in the corner or closet area. Yet, there was no one present. I got up and quickly opened the closet door. No one was there … or in the hallway, or outside my window. Yes, I was sure it was not my imagination. I heard a loud baritone man's voice say, "Stop throwing your pearls to swine". It was quite unbelievable, yet real. I knew this was a message from spirit. I knew what the message meant. I had to permanently rid Nathan from my life.

Facing My Ugly Monster

"Until you make the unconscious conscious, it will direct your life and you will call it fate."
~ Dr. Carl G. Jung

There is no way to sugarcoat our ugliness we find inside ourselves. It is not in our hearts that we hold this disfigurement, but in our subconscious. Carved into us like the pattern on a leaf or your own fingerprint, the abuse you endured becomes an involuntary reaction to cope in situations where you don't know what else to do.

I was having trouble with my oldest daughter and striking out at her physically on occasion. She could be very sneaky, argumentative and quite a persistent handful at times. Until this day, I had smacked her in the face or spanked her rear end. However, one day it culminated in a horrible, shameful, abusive event where I found myself yelling at my oldest child and pinning her down on the kitchen floor choking her momentarily. Abruptly, I stopped and the red hot anger turned to tears and apologies.

Realizing that I was repeating some of what had been done to me, I broke down and knew this had to change. I knew my behavior was out of control and wrong. Worse yet, I couldn't erase the pain or impact it had on my daughter. Following the family tradition of trying to control others with violence, I was acting out my past with my mother and my current situation with Nathan.

My bright, beautiful and frightened girl did what she should have done. She picked up the phone and called someone once the incident had ended. Who did she call? She phoned her grandmother, my abuser, who promptly notified the authorities.

I was angry that my mother called authorities on me. Of all the people to do this! All those years when no one came to my rescue, even when I told others what was going on. Even when I begged to come live with them to get out of that house, yet no one would agree. But I had bigger things to deal with because Child Protective Service was now at my door.

I had real skin in the game. I was caught between being a victim of abuse and an abuser myself. Popped like a rubber band that has been stretched too far, I had to face this about myself. I made an instant decision. I will not be her. I am not her and I won't act like her. A more mature parental way of discipline had to be found. I was determined not to let this madness of abuse continue in my family.

When you have a pattern of reacting in a certain way set into a portion of your brain, it is easy to let that be the first thing that happens when there is conflict of any sort. No one had given me the right set of parental tools, including my father who took a long time to lose his temper but was also violent when he did.

My biggest focus became being a better mother – one who knew how to discipline her children without resorting to abuse. And it wasn't easy. Not only did I have to learn new strategies, I was dealing now with a child who had been conditioned to think I did not really mean business or was not serious unless I showed anger.

What about my beautiful girl? I felt so horrible for the hurt I had caused her – the trauma of having mom suddenly turn to monster. Whether she was old enough or understood completely, I sat her down and told her everything. She knew her grandmother was abusive. She had experienced that herself at times with hair brush incidents and other things when she had stayed with her. But she did not know my childhood in its entirety. I told her what had happened to me in detail. I promised her that things were going to change and I went through all the motions necessary to effect that change quickly.

Through my counseling and reading, I continually gained more insight into what good parenting looked like. I began talking to other mothers I admired to get ideas on handling misbehavior. Gradually at first and then picking up momentum, I began changing and stopped behaving that way. It took time and thinking ahead. When a behavior issue arose, I had to mentally slow things down and choose to respond differently. Constantly being mentally focused on responding differently to childhood antics was sometimes overwhelming. I would miss the mark at times, but I kept at it and wanted to make sure I was nothing like my mother when it came to my reactions with my children.

My child never heard phrases from me like "I wish you were never born" or "You're nothing but a burden to me." But she was not dealt with fairly and correctly as I smacked her or when we had the incident on the kitchen floor. What I was doing was so wrong on every level and I had to own up to it and stop this crazy pattern that had been set into my memory bank.

I learned to set boundaries for my children and put in place non-combative penalties for their misbehavior such as loss of privileges, toys, etc. I gave in too easily with their persistence of wanting those items they temporarily lost back. So, I had to learn consistency. And I had done these things prior, but lacked the measured follow-through to say "No, you won't get that back until such and such date", because that required more of me and my energy. But this was a better way. I had to learn it and then do it.

I was becoming a more conscious mother, a better human who realized that if I did not change right now, I was going to impact my children in such a negative way. I knew before Child Protective Services arrived that I had crossed a significant line. I knew this was not the real me and something had to be done to keep this pattern from occurring in my family.

If you're fortunate, one of these days you are going to watch your grandchildren come into this world. How do we want them to be treated? It starts with me. It doesn't end with me, but it started there and I had the power to fix it.

Yes, it stung to have my own abuser call the authorities and play "good mom". But it didn't matter who made the call. I needed cold water poured on my head. My awakening would help save my children. Here I had all this so called spirituality that seemed like the core of me, but I found myself that day acting like an animal.

As much as I needed to learn to be a better parent, I also needed to start learning to mother myself. Those open sores were my point of pain that would direct me toward healing. Transmuting my anger into compassion seemed arduous, yet occurred naturally over time by staying a course that was self directed and assisted by others helping me.

Shame, unworthiness and feelings of not being good enough lie at the bottom of it all. But I did not realize this at the time. These lower vibratory emotions were dragging me down and drowning me in an internal misery I covered up with busyness and denial.

Breaking patterns and facing the ugliness was my only hope for true transformation. There was no way I could begin to give myself or my children what was needed – what was missing – until I did this work. I had looked for someone else to love me, but that wasn't working out. I was looking at progress or getting ahead at work to fulfill me, but it didn't. It was an admirable thing, but it was a band-aid on a gaping wound.

That day of abuse toward my child was a pivotal point. I dedicated myself to being the best mom I could be. Shame is a teacher at times. It shows us what must not be repeated again because it always reveals a crime against ourselves or others. Yet, it should only be a reminder – a placeholder in our psyche and not something we internalize to be the true "us". If it were the true "us", we would feel no shame. We would be psychopaths.

I was honest and shared my reasons for why I had been abusive with my daughter, trying to make her understand that it was not a reflection of her, but me. I still occasionally apologize to her for any mistreatment or harsh words that happened. It is embarrassing, but I own it. I corrected it, making sure she understood the reasons for my poor reactions and how special she was and is to me. It doesn't fix the wrong, but it made it easier for both of us to move forward as two hearts that will always be entwined as mother and daughter.

We must keep in mind that our parenting style to our children will be their knee jerk reaction with their offspring. If they want to improve or make it different, that same process of analyzing what they are doing and changing will need to be implemented to break the chain. We should be mindful that the way we rear our children will affect the way our grandchildren will be raised. It is a chain of impact unless someone has courage to break the patterns and create a new way of childrearing and loving discipline.

Now, I still raised my voice at times – especially to get teen daughter number two out of bed in the morning when she would not respond to multiple attempts to wake her. I wasn't a perfect mom after that. I was a human mother trying to be the best at the job I could be and learning more constantly. That's all we can ask of ourselves. But I stopped using physical means to discipline. No more slaps in the face and certainly no choking on the floor.

I was in the grocery recently and a mother had her two children along. The older boy who was probably about four years old was pinching the younger girl who appeared to be a toddler. The mother told him that if he did not stop pinching her, she was going to spank him when they got home. We often hear this and may have said it ourselves. While I thought it was good and necessary that she come to the younger child's rescue, I also saw the irony in it. She was saying if you don't stop pinching, I'm going to start hitting you.

We have to find ways to instill empathy in our children, making them realize that what they do to others has impact. Effective ways must be found where we are not teaching children that violence fixes violence or misbehavior. Teaching children about boundaries is difficult as they will test them. Showing them we just do not do certain behaviors and halting it by some means that is more educational is ideal.

One idea we used with our younger daughter at the store was to allow her to pick out something she wanted that was on the "approved" list – that list consisting of affordable and appropriate. If she began misbehaving, the item was removed from the cart (or threatened to be removed) and she would not receive it. We had some meltdowns and fits in the store at times and did not give into it.

It is very challenging to be a parent. Usually, we come into the care of our children equipped only with the skills we have learned thus far. Those practices may not always be so healthy. It's something we have to look at in our society to become more peaceful, loving and cooperative.

My middle sister tells the story of how our mother made her eat bologna which she hated. She sat silently at the table and refused to eat it, crying and begging mom. In frustration, our mother finally began screaming, pulling my sister's hair and forcing it into her throat. She threw up and my mother grabbed her from the chair, beating her and stuck her head under the faucet in the bathroom in hot water. She was less than ten years old.

True to form, my mother took her shopping the next day for new things and never mentioned anything about the incident. She was conditioning my sister and buying silence.

All children are without defense unless someone comes to their rescue against people who can turn into monsters at a moment's notice. I was out of the house, living on my own, or I would have. Yet, I am sure this would not have happened if I had been present. Again, these people do have some control.

In the beginning, I was only going to put a couple of paragraphs about my bad parenting. I woke up at 3am one night knowing I had to be totally authentic, even if it was adding more things that were embarrassing and did not show me in a good light. I knew that was an aspect of myself that I conquered and not the real me that wants to express itself. It is my hope that we can always face our inner monsters and transform them into something else. This is true evolution.

Healing

"Healing doesn't mean the damage never existed. It means the damage no longer controls our lives."
~ Bruce Lipton, PhD

When I was not working, I spent the next few years immersed in my spiritual studies and self-help psychology books. I found a social worker to counsel me and she charged based upon my income. Initially, she wanted me to do quite a bit of journaling and dream work. I resisted this, telling her I would and then making excuses when she wanted to know how that was going. I was busy and often staying that way purposely to avoid looking closely at things.

In my weekly sessions with her, we primarily focused on Nathan and why I was with him. I know we spoke about my difficulties with my mom, but we did not talk in depth about the Smitty experience. Still covered in a sheath of shame, it was hit on lightly with little to no details. Most of our conversations revolved around why I had not broken this off permanently with Nathan since I knew the relationship was not good for me.

My counselor recommended books to read throughout therapy and I began with books on codependency such as Melody Beattie's *Codependent No More*. Another book I read was *Women Who Love Too Much* by Robin Norwood.

She also wanted me to read *The Courage to Heal: A Guide For Women Survivors of Sexual Abuse* by Ellen Bass and Laura Davis. It was a large book with a separate workbook that accompanied it. I felt embarrassed to purchase it at the bookstore. I lived in such denial believing I did not have issues to heal over sexual abuse. I saw my early childhood life with my mother as the only abuse I needed to address.

Reading this book on sexual abuse, hearing the stories of people tortured since infancy, this was not me. I told myself that I was okay and stopped reading halfway through. I could not see myself even as a survivor of any type of sexual abuse. I lived in a denial that was thick as a stone wall.

Yet my sexuality had been compromised. I just didn't realize it. I never experienced an orgasm until my mid-twenties and that was with the help of a small vibrator my girlfriend had recommended I get. I had so much control over my body functions that I could never relax into sex enough for an actual orgasm to occur. It took a tremendous amount of stimulation for me to achieve same via the vibrator.

Until my first orgasm, I thought I was having them. Feeling the sensations that come with the joining of a man and woman, I just assumed that was it. The "fireworks" going off in someone's head and other notions from girl talk and movies was something I thought was overblown or exaggerated. So, after having borne three children, I still had not experienced an orgasm until I did so with the help of a small vibrator. I never completely finished the book or workbook on sexual abuse. Finding myself thinking I just did not need that help, the stories were disturbing and made me feel depressed.

Although I had engaged in meditation many times before, my mind stayed too busy to attempt it now. I think the silence had become uncomfortable for me. Still, I worked on reprogramming myself with more positive material and fell asleep almost every night to a guided meditation. I was working on things in the waking and sleeping state. The changes must have still been very small for me at this time because I was so far from where I would be later in my recovery process.

I had allowed Nathan to beat down my self-esteem in certain ways and I was slowly beginning to regain it, but I was not where I needed to be. Because I was afraid of being alone, I would often let him back into my life. This is common in toxic relationships. We become so adapted and bonded to the abusive nature of the relationship that when we are without it, we cannot stand the separation. Finding ourselves remembering the good times we had with that person, we wonder if we have blown things out of proportion from the last blow-up and question our decision.

Other reasons I continued this on again/off again dance with him was that I sometimes felt I was depriving my daughter of her father. Jealousy about him being with someone else would also keep me thinking of him and eventually seeing him. It would take time for me to feel no jealousy of another woman being with Nathan. That day did eventually come and instead, I felt sorry for her.

Still occasionally seeing Nathan, I was not "cured" of that. However, I saw him less often as time went by and it became a rare event. Often, he would initiate the contact and he used our daughter as an excuse more than a few times. Now when I relented and allowed him into my life, I was much more analytical about why. Why was I on this wheel with him and why would I even be attracted to his personality in the first place? Sure, he had very charming ways at times but for the most part, he was a true loser and abusive. He was also a psychic vampire, meaning that he had an aura about himself that sucked the life force and energy out of those around him. Once he had made you feel horrible, he felt satisfied in some grim way. I observed this many times.

Others often described Nathan as a dark cloud when he entered the room. I am not sure he realized he was doing this. Although he was cunning and smart, I don't really think he could get outside of himself to feel what others felt around him. It was one of the main reasons his music would go nowhere. Other musicians shunned him because he was just so difficult to be around.

I had met Nathan at twenty-three and now here I was struggling to break free at thirty-two or thirty-three. Since our daughter had a relationship with his mother and sister, this complicated things. Obviously, I was also afraid to be totally alone.

Frustrated that I had not told him goodbye forever, I took it out on myself and my own inability to control my impulses. Often, I found myself waking up with this anger that I didn't fully understand. It was all the emotions I had been repressing. I knew something needed to be done to fix myself. It was because of my two daughters that my inner rage and depression led me to seek outside help from many sources. I was driven to be the best I could be as a parent. I had to find a way to pull myself together. Yet, I was still really only in coping mode. I was not thriving as an individual.

Believing I could do all this inner work on my own, I stopped seeing my counselor. Honestly, I did feel she and I had reached a point where I was not benefiting enough from the sessions. Yet, I continued allowing Nathan back into my life. We would be okay for several weeks or even three months, but then it would fall apart.

When I think back to why it would never work, there were many reasons. His infidelity and lies, the steady stream of put-downs, not helping out financially yet often living at my house, wanting to keep me from having friends, and negative draining nature are just a few.

During the times he was away from me and my girls, I felt lighter and happier. Yet, I also experienced that nagging inner rage that I would wake up with at times. I did not know what the anger was about or where it was coming from inside me. Simultaneously, I had bouts of depression and thoughts of suicide at times. My girls – I could not do that to them. They were literally what drove me to do better, change, and be the best I could be.

I decided to try a different therapy approach with a psychiatrist which my work insurance would pay for. The doctor put me on Prozac for depression, although I assured him that I would not be killing myself, but I had been honest that I had thought of it at times. There was just no way I would do anything like that. I had two girls I loved dearly and would do nothing to harm myself which would hurt them in turn.

I had weekly sessions with the doctor and really felt like we were not accomplishing much, but I was without knowing it. I was being forced to talk about all the things that had been buried in a deeper way now than I had with my counselor. Those subjects were now out in the open with my doctor. We talked about my childhood and my subsequent kidnapping, along with what was transpiring at that time in my life.

Often, professionals do not say much during your sessions. It can seem as if you are doing all the work and, in a way, you are. Yet their expertise is in drawing out of you that which needs to be looked at and faced. Professionals also have a way of opening you up to look at new directions for your life. This can be changes you are currently making and will make in the future.

I visited my parents after work one day and my mother asked me to come outside so she could talk to me alone. We sat on a small bench and she asked me why I was seeing a psychiatrist. I told her it was because I was depressed, sometimes angry and that I had issues I needed to deal with from the past. She began pleading with me to stop seeing the doctor. My mom insisted this was just dragging up things from the past and probably making me worse instead of better. I told her it did feel like that sometimes, but I had to do this for now.

She began crying and told me that she knew she had been cruel to me as a child. She said she was sorry and wished she could fix it. I found myself feeling sorry for her and how distraught she was. She again begged me to stop seeing the psychiatrist but I told her I had to for now. It would not be forever. It was quite apparent toward the end of our conversation that she was afraid of being found out. She did not want some doctor knowing about our family history. This had more to do with her feeling fear around the idea of being found out than actual remorse. Although I won't pretend to know her mind entirely, she may have felt quite sorry. It was no different than her coming into my room at night, stroking my hair, crying and saying she was sorry. It was the same.

Who else did not like me seeing the psychiatrist? Nathan didn't like it nor did he want me to see my girlfriends. He was hypercritical of each of them. He wanted to isolate me so that the abusive relationship could continue without influence from other people who would constantly try to talk to me and show me how detrimental it was. I remember him telling me on several occasions that these girlfriends of mine were just jealous – especially if they were not in a relationship.

As time went on, I did not like how the antidepressant affected me. I noticed I was not the same. Specifically, I seemed to not care about things as much. It was as if my emotions were dulled and while that may have worked for the mild depression, it did not work for the things that used to bring me joy. I loved doing a lot of projects on the weekends with my girls and nothing seemed fun anymore. Abruptly taking myself off of the antidepressant, I began feeling everything very intensely for a short time.

I found myself emotionally distraught and crying at any little thing. One day, instead of going to work, I took a sick day off. My girls were at school and I spent the day going through all sorts of old letters, photographs and keepsakes in a chest I had stored them in. I did a lot of crying and I believe it was beneficial.

I continued reading my psychology books and got a wild hair, painting my living room walls a brilliant orange and then feathered in gold and other fall palette colors. It was bold, but it reminded me of the same colors of the sugar maple tree outside in the fall. I realized later that orange signifies courage and healing from trauma related to second chakra issues. I was on the right track instinctively without knowing it.

When my insurance ran out and I had maxed out my paid visits to the psychiatrist, I was not dismayed at all. I started relying on my intuition to guide me to what I needed to do next to move toward further healing. Joining group therapy with other survivors of abuse assisted me greatly, as well as staying on the codependent issues I carried with me.

By now, I had put the connections together. I could see why I would be attracted to Nathan in the first place. He was a strange conglomeration of Smitty and my mother. What a combination the universe served up for me to learn from. I realized that Nathan wasn't the problem. I was. Don't get me wrong. He had severe personality disorders, yet his problems were only mine if I allowed them to be.

What did it take for me to finally make the cut and not be in a relationship with him? It took coming to the edge. I did not seek help for myself or stop seeing him when he was being verbally abusive, emotionally mistreating me, taking advantage of my good will, or even held against the wall in a chokehold. I sought help when the pain inside me became so intolerable that it turned into a rage and accompanying depression. When I had thoughts of ending my life, that's when I surrendered. That is when I was willing to seek help from the psychiatrist and I am very glad I did. Even though it only lasted for a few months of weekly visits, I was able to make major headway with healing. Finally, I had the courage and a support system of other people in place to end the relationship with Nathan.

On my own, I began listening to motivational material of all types from Tony Robbins, Louise Hay and Dr. Wayne Dyer. I surrounded myself with girlfriends, all who knew my struggles with Nathan and encouraged me to stay clear of him.

I spent considerable time exploring the idea of the negative ego or subconscious and breaking free as best I could. I had allowed certain portions of my brain to constantly hold me back, repeating to me everything I was not or could not do. I began connecting mentally with my higher self who knew I was capable of better. This was lengthy study that spanned over years and continues today.

We all have a part of us that wants to rule our life with its negative comments on who we are. It consistently attempts to tell us what we cannot do or be. I began letting it have its voice, but making it smaller with continual affirmations that took the opposite stance.

During this time of healing, I met my higher self while in a deep meditation and this was a life changing event. I connected with her inside a dark cave, a scene I had concocted within my own mind. As I entered the cave, I had no idea what my higher self would be like. She was illuminated with light and had a human form, but it was like looking at a projection. Her hair and skin glowed with light, along with her green eyes that held deep pools of emotion that felt so loving – a love I had not felt ever before.

My task was to ask her one question -- what was the most important thing I needed to know about my life? Seeing her with my mind's eye and hearing what few, but important, words she had to say to me was something I will never forget. She spoke mentally to me, "You need to love yourself more." Basking in the unconditional love I felt from her, I accepted her answer readily. Later upon reflection, my analytical mind kicked in and I felt her answer was too simplistic. This made me doubt the entire encounter as something I made up in my mind and I remember being a tad agitated by it. Yet, time has proven that loving myself enough is my challenge.

I had continued my metaphysical studies over these years with a wide variety of things like crystals, tarot, and astrology. I had been an avid student of herbs for years and had experimented in my kitchen, making my own little remedies and cosmetics at times. Frustrated with the shelf life of my home-made creations, I began selling a line of skin care that was plant-based and very beneficial as a side job.

I spent time absorbing Shakti Gawain's books, *Creative Visualization* and *Living in the Light*. I studied many different forms of esoteric sciences. Reading glasses became necessary with all the late nights I was keeping with my studies.

What I learned about myself to never be repeated was that it was most unwise to be in a relationship with someone who does not view you in a high manner or treat you with great respect. Love is only what our maturity level dictates. It is ever changing with our knowledge and experience. Our capacity to give and receive love ebbs and flows as we can only do that in direct relation to how we are feeling about ourselves. I also learned to listen better to what people say about others and what their actions and deeds reflect prior to becoming their friend or lover. I've often told my girls to listen how a guy talks about his mother. How he treats his mother is how he will treat you.

I also learned to never declare myself completely healed from those early experiences, as much as I would like to be. It comes back at odd times -- as if you were on a carousel of life, riding your favorite horse. All the sites you pass while riding it are lovely. Suddenly, the ride turns to a view that is disgusting and horrible and you see it. Shocked, you thought it would go away, never to return -- especially after all the work you did to clean up the area and make it disappear. Yet, it is there staring you briefly in the face and you get off the ride, clean it up some more, only to get back on and pass it later again.

Where was the girl who thought she was brave enough to sing on stage with Tom Petty that night if she could have managed the opportunity? I had such an old story playing in my head now of "not good enough". It only took Nathan reflecting those ideas and feelings to me a few times to put my dreams on hold. If I had remained more confident, I would have pursued things further. If I had continued to grab the bull by the horns, invoked carpe diem, my entire life could have taken a different turn.

When you managed to have that kind of face-to-face meeting with someone and an invitation to possibly connect again through your music, letting both of them slide away seemed wasteful. You could not help but look back with all those "what ifs". Yet, I have had and I do have a great life. Truly, no one can keep your good from you. We are all capable of manifesting great things for ourselves through our imagination, will and intent, coupled with action.

The key to erasing shame or feelings of failure is to actually forgive yourself for the role you have played in it all. Forgive those that participated with you as they have served as catalysts and teachers. It does not excuse their behavior and I believe they accumulate their own burdens of karma. Yet, that is not for us to judge or revel in.

Just acknowledging that we have the power to be different by forgiving our parts in our "mistake" is liberating. Think of your physical body for a moment. All of the cells that make up this body vehicle that you inhabit are different and new as compared to one year ago. Each day, millions of cells are dying off, replaced by brand new ones which you have the power through your God given gifts of creation and thought to program how you see fit.

The dilemma is that we do not typically think this way. We often allow the old patterns in our subconscious to control the show. Instead of telling this portion of ourselves "Quiet, we are playing a new movie now. Everyone is tired of that old story." Yes, it may be a dramatic blockbuster, but now we are into the next sequel – the one with happy endings where the hero or heroine rises out of the ashes like a phoenix.

If we can see our stories as just that --- old and worn out, tried on like clothes you wore when you were eight years old and no longer fit, we are on our way to creating a new story and destiny for ourselves.

The relationship I had with this antisocial personality was long lasting. I had a gift from it though: my baby girl who has grown into a beautiful, mature woman that adds a lot to the world. Nathan's gift to me was that he served as a strong catalyst to make me start learning to love myself and seek help.

Being in love with a guy who is often distant and does not love you like you love him is not honoring yourself. Respect yourself too much for that and, if you find yourself unable to peel yourself away, get some counseling to find out why.

I also learned that when you pull away and discard what is not in your highest interest and make moves toward what is good for you and all concerned, miracles begin to happen.

Little things began to occur that were small synchronicities and intuitive moments propelling me in new directions that were healthier. My healing was progressing and it is only in looking back now that I can see how this happened. While inside the experience of healing, I felt stagnant at times. Yet, things were changing and happening each day.

My dreams took on more significance and I often would spend time visualizing what I wanted my life to look like. I became more forgiving of myself through my spiritual practice. I accepted that we are all here to learn and, if perfect, would not be here at all. I viewed this life and planet earth as a place to really focus down on lessons my soul needed so that I could progress and move to higher levels.

Skating On Thin Ice

"If you don't like the road you're walking, start paving another one."
~ Dolly Parton

Nathan had been absent from my life for awhile. He showed up at my house unannounced, as usual, on Martin Luther King Day during the winter of 1992. I am sure he knew the kids would be out of school. He was in his charming personality mode and offered to take his daughter and I ice skating. She had never been and I had loved ice skating as a teen but had never taken my daughters.

I was smart enough now to know to say NO. But, I didn't. I agreed to go thinking it would be harmless. Once we arrived at the outdoor rink, we noticed the ice was not very smooth after a once around the rails with our daughter who was brand new to this. The ice had large chunks embedded into its surface which would normally be taken care of by the machines they ran over the rink. We wondered if the guards would call a time out soon and the machine would be there on the ice to get things smooth, but this never happened.

Skating was challenging with the bumpy ice, but we continued on for awhile. We were going to go around the rink just one more time and I decided to go fast. My skate hit a large chunk of ice and my body was sent flying. My right skate was turned completely and locked in with the ice chunk while my body twisted the opposite direction. I heard something pop before I landed. I came down hard on my right ankle.

Once down on the ice, I began feeling nauseous and knew I was seriously hurt. The guards helped me off the ice and I asked Nathan to go get my car and drive it as close as possible. He kept telling me I was being a big baby and that I probably sprained my ankle. I knew I was in such severe pain that it was something more.

Our daughter was probably a bit traumatized from watching and hearing all of this. She was seven years old. I could hardly keep from crying on the way to the hospital. He kept berating me, telling me that I was not hurt as bad as I thought.

At the hospital, they x-rayed and found I had shattered the lower portion of my right tibia and it would not heal on its own. I would need surgery. I had a second fracture to my right heel bone that was a clean break and would, thankfully, heal on its own. Nathan was a little surprised to hear this. Since I would need to meet with a surgeon, they placed a temporary cast on my right leg. Nathan drove me home in my car.

I felt quite helpless as I could not get up the exterior steps to the front or side door of my house without help. I could not drive. The hospital gave me some pills for pain and I went to sleep. In the morning, I phoned the orthopedic surgeon they had recommended and made an appointment. I was able to get in that afternoon. Nathan again drove me there and he still acted like I was a bit of a baby about my injuries. He went into the exam room with me and the doctor put my x-rays up on the screen. He showed us how one bone was shattered and said that it would need assistance in growing back which would require placing a wire inside for the new bone to grow to. He said the break of the heel bone was clean and would grow back on its own fine. There were also torn ligaments that could take awhile to heal also.

He then took off the temporary cast and my leg had huge black blisters on it. Nathan was aghast when he saw it. I tried not to look too closely. He called them fracture blisters and said they would go away. He put a new cast on and scheduled me for surgery. He wanted the swelling to go down some before he operated on my ankle.

After surgery, I was put into a more permanent cast and that leg elevated in my hospital bed where I would spend the night. My youngest daughter spent the night with Nathan's mother and my oldest one who was now fifteen would spend the night at her girlfriend's house. I was given regular doses of morphine and waiting four hours between each shot was not enough to cut the extreme pain I was in. It felt like someone was standing at the end of my bed with a blowtorch on my leg.

During the night, I dreamed I saw my oldest daughter driving about in my car with her friend. I awoke and was disturbed by this so I called Nathan who I knew would be up in the middle of the night. I asked him to go by my house and see if my car was in the drive. He called back later saying it was gone.

Once daylight came, I called the girl's mother of the house my daughter was supposed to be staying at. She had no idea I was in the hospital recovering from surgery. The girls had told her they were spending the night at my house and she assumed I was there. So, this was something else to deal with when I got home. Once I spoke with my daughter, she admitted she took the car out and dented the rear end of it, along with side swiping a couple of cars on a busy street.

I did not know if the police would be showing up at my door looking for me now, thinking I had side swiped cars. At least I could tell them I was in the hospital that night, but what about my daughter? She had saved a little over two hundred dollars and I required her to give it to me for the dent in the car and whatever else I did not know about. She felt it unfair, but something had to be done to make her think twice about her illegal actions.

The surgeon told me in advance that I would be in a wheelchair for six weeks and could not have a walking cast. It was a major adjustment and I was off work for several weeks until I could drive.

In my mind I kept wishing I had never gone ice skating with Nathan. I felt this was just another example the universe was giving me to stay away from him. Once I returned home, Nathan was now using my broken bones as an excuse to stay at my house and mooch off me under the guise of helping me. I had felt a new peace during the time we had not been in contact. Having him with me day and night now was really hindering me. He was extremely foul mouthed and negative.

I had three places I could be: the couch, wheelchair or my bed. As I would lie on the couch watching television, he would criticize every show I liked or make rude comments about the actors. He would argue with the television when I watched the news, pacing the living room floor spouting off about "the government".

Despite the fact that I needed a lot of help, I reached a limit one evening with him and asked him to leave. With my cordless telephone nestled beside me on the couch, I told him I needed him to leave now because his energy was too much for me and I felt I could not heal. In case he started anything physical with me, I was prepared to call the police.

I had gained a new appreciation for walking since I could not. I often lie there thinking about people who were living their lives this way. What challenges they faced. This was temporary and I would heal, but I had to be away from him. And I was not just thinking of healing my bones.

Now that I was grounded at home, I had much more time to spend thinking about what I really wanted in life and looking at things I still covered up with my busyness. I spent time using creative visualization techniques and doing affirmations. Good changes were coming and, this time, the synchronicities would be attached to those lighter, happier moments instead of turmoil or tragedy.

Rebuilding Camelot

"There are ignorant priests and ignorant people, who are all too ready to cry sorcery if a woman is only a little wiser than they are!"

"I should know, for I am Morgain Le Fay, priestess of the Isle of Avalon, where the ancient religion of the Mother Goddess is born."

~ Marion Zimmer Bradley, *The Mists of Avalon*

My life took on a duality as I spent weekdays preparing documents and proposals in my secretarial capacity and my nights immersed in the deeper study of metaphysics and my other interests. One night, I had a dream that was very vivid and real. When I am having a significant or precognitive dream, I can always tell because I remember it very well and it is almost like someone turned up the color hues on it. There is much emotion tied to the dream and it will stick with me, sometimes for weeks. It is difficult to relate how important I know a dream to be. I can only say that the emotions fueling it are a tremendous clue. A few times, I have interacted with a blonde haired, blue eyed man in my dream that is talking with me and he is always a teacher or authority figure of some kind.

In this dream, it was a beautiful day with blue skies, sunshine and cotton white clouds – a perfect sky. I was standing on a hill under a tree with this blonde haired, blue eyed man. We were both watching what was going on down in the valley. Buildings were being erected. Workers were busy on the project and they looked like tiny ants from where we stood.

I asked the man standing with me, "What are they doing?" "We are rebuilding Camelot", he said. I looked at him and our eyes locked in a way that was not like lovers, but like transference of two people who know each other as one – something beyond lovers. I knew that when he said 'we' that it included me. Yes, we were rebuilding Camelot and there was an excitement and happiness that surrounded the idea. Yet, there was also much work to be done. I felt that as we parted and I awoke.

All my waking day, the dream stayed on my mind. I had no idea what rebuilding Camelot meant. I knew this was a message dream and it had some importance but I could not make sense of it. When one of these important dreams gets into my being, I cannot let it go. It becomes like a tiny tick latched on and sucking the blood out of me. The only way I can remove it is to solve the puzzle of the dream.

I phoned a clairvoyant I knew from my church and asked her if she knew what this could mean. She said she had no idea. She did mention that she knew a lady named Lori who believed she lived a past life during that fabled time of Camelot, King Arthur and such. She gave me her phone number and I called her.

Following the trail like a hound dog, trying to answer this riddle, I could never actually speak to Lori when I phoned her. I would always speak with one of her children who were extremely polite. Finally, I did speak with her husband. He said that Lori was out of town but she would be back Friday because she was teaching a class on Saturday. I asked him where the class was and he gave me the place. I phoned the organization and signed myself up for the Saturday class.

Excitedly, I phoned my best friend Anna, telling her about the class and maybe I could finally talk with this lady Lori. "What is the class?" she inquired. "Flower essences and healing," I replied. "Oh, I would like that too" my friend said excitedly. So, I phoned and made a reservation for Anna also.

The class was small and we met in a quiet room large enough only for the long rectangle table where we sat. Lori was at the head of the table and I was sitting about in the middle on the left side of Anna. Lori was a petite woman with brunette hair that seemed to fall with a natural wave or curl. Her hair was mid-length, neither short nor long. She wore a dress and appeared as if she could have been addressing a local woman's club. She had a calm demeanor, yet a strong presence at the same time. I was not sure of her age, but guessed it to be early forties based upon her life experiences and ages of her children that she shared with us. However, she looked very ageless in a beautiful way. In total, there were ten of us - a small class and an intimate setting.

A lady sitting across from Anna and I was making gestures and body language throughout Lori's presentation that suggested she was having a hard time coping emotionally for some reason. I don't think I've ever seen anyone act like that in a class situation before or since that time. It was very intrusive and affected our ability to pay attention to Lori.

Suddenly, Lori said very softly, "Let me take just a moment with Jenny". She walked over behind Jenny and put her arms around her very lovingly. Everything Lori did had this loving ambience that is difficult to describe. She was gentle in her mannerisms, yet you could see strength in her that was confident, but without arrogance. She bent down and whispered in the ear of the distraught woman and hugged her – not a quick hug but a long, enduring one that seemed to hold meaning. Jenny's facial expression changed as she relaxed and appeared fine the rest of the lecture.

This floored me! Because I was of the nature to have told Jenny it was time for her to go outside the room and pull herself together, but no, Lori loved her and the lady joined in with the rest of us and we were all happy.

Yet, it was the way Lori did it. Such slow elegance combined with her soft Southern accent and gentle ways. I admired Lori and I wanted to be like her. I wanted what she had. To be able to take someone and flip them 180 degrees so instantaneously when they had seemed so out of sorts one minute before was remarkable.

While soft music from *The Fairy Ring* by Mike Rowland played in the background, Lori went on with our lesson plan and explained to us many intricate details of working with flower essences, including utilizing the Bach flower remedies.

Lori explained how she had become involved in all of this work. Formerly a nurse, she was in an auto accident wherein she had a head injury. She stated that as soon as the wreck happened, she could hear someone speaking to her. Her vision was fuzzy at first and she could not see fully who it was but as this person came into view, he introduced himself to her as St. Germain. She said he was one of her guides and she now hears and sees him all the time. Lori stressed he was not the only guide, but a very prominent one for her right now.

Having experienced her own synchronistic warnings or predictions, she knew the car wreck was going to happen prior. It was just a time when wheels were literally set into motion and things were occurring that would propel her towards a different destiny. Some of Lori's family were also injured in the accident. After recovering from her injuries, she did not return to nursing.

Lori found herself being attracted to working with flowers. She and her husband owned a small farm in Kentucky and she began growing a lot of beautiful varieties. She learned to dry and preserve them, later using the flowers to adorn straw hats for ladies to purchase and wear to the Kentucky Derby and elsewhere.

She made quite a name for herself with her hats because that's how ladies are when they find a product they like, it goes viral and every socialite must have one. At the time of our class, the trend was waning and she did not sell as many hats as before. Yet, she did not seem to care about that. To her, it was just a fluke that she had made something everyone was crazy about.

She told us that each of us has an individual flower essence that we match with and that this can change as we metamorphose in our journey. Her flower was Queen Anne's Lace. This plant grows naturally like a weed on my property and I always let it grow and think of Lori. She was the epitome of a flower essence – a substance that is so gentle in its presentation, but so powerful in its signature that it leaves.

She also assigned a particular gem stone to each of us as well. Anna's was lapis lazuli and mine was fluorite. I thought Anna's was more beautiful than mine and I secretly wished for hers. Yet, I came to understand that my fluorite stone was something that I needed.

Lori said she chose fluorite for me because it would help keep me safe and grounded. "You're an astral traveler." How would she know this? I wasn't sure I was such a thing, even though I knew I had a lot of dream activity.

Not conscious of it at the time, I am a person who can travel out of body and intuit things through sleep. My dream work is one of the most important things I indulge in. Lori said that fluorite would enhance astral travel and keep me safe with its grounding attributes.

We had been through a great many flower essences and understood how they worked on a vibrational level to assist in emotional healing; thus lending recovery for physical ailments as well. Lori had briefly touched on the powerful attributes of stones which also work off resonance or vibration. Lori ended the learning session by stating that she would like to perform a healing or tuning on each of us individually.

Retreating to a small hallway outside of this room, Lori placed a chair in the middle of the hall. She called us each out one at a time and would shut the door and be with each person privately. I was not sure exactly what she was doing but I did not feel any trepidation until I saw Anna return from her healing experience with Lori.

Anna emerged from her solo session with Lori, tears streaming down her face. My friend continued to cry a river of tears. I kept giving her tissues, trying to console her while waiting my turn. I asked, "What did she do to you?" Anna could not explain it in words but kept assuring me she was okay. I totally saw that it was a good cry and not to worry. I was tentative about walking out of this room into the next to receive my session with Lori. I just wanted to ask her about Camelot and not end up in some strange display of emotion.

Lori emitted love from her entire persona. However, I was totally amazed at how she also emitted the aroma of flowers. Lori could blow the smell of flowers from her breath and she would do this in a face to face position with you while she was gently holding onto your shoulders. It was healing, unbelievable, yet real and incredible. When asked how she could do this, she said the ability came to her later after working with the flowers for so long on her farm and study of the flower essences. She felt it was a gift or blessing given to her to use on behalf of others.

Lori motioned for me to sit in the chair which was in the middle of the hall area. As soon as I sat down, I felt compelled to ask her about Camelot and told her my dream. She said to me, "You are Igraine. You were King Arthur's mother and mine too. I was Morgaine". This was very surprising but it did sound like the Camelot dream was finding some connection. I told Lori, "It feels like you are my mother, my teacher." Lori said, "We change roles in various lifetimes. We are from the same soul group, and these are aspects of our personalities. You hold that archetype and I hold mine but we were not necessarily those exact people." She asked me if I understood and I nodded affirmatively, but was really just digesting the information. I did not totally get it but I allowed the conversation to continue without sticking on that point.

Recently, I heard this concept related another way. *Archetypical synergistic resonance* is a term invented by Jeffrey Mishlove, PhD. To this parapsychologist, it means that you may feel you were Cleopatra in a past life. Indeed, you may have synchronistic dreams and events that happen in this life to lead you to this belief. Yet, there may be a part of you that does not want to allow your ego to buy into this as a fact. Instead, you resonate with this character in a very real way and fit the archetype of this historical person. Others can also feel they were Cleopatra, having similar synergistic resonance with the archetype. This may be a partial explanation for why more than one person can resonate with an archetypical or historical person.

Lori urged me to read *The Mists of Avalon*. "In that book," she said, "you will find a large part of your purpose. Your purpose involves elegantly bridging gaps between traditional Christianity and the spiritual life path. You also should read two more books because all three are part of your journey." She recommended *The Metaphysics of Sex* and *Wheels of Life*. I later visited my favorite bookstore picking up these books. She also said that St. Germain was my guide as well. I was not sure how this could work. How could St. Germain be her guide and mine? I just listened and took in the information to think about.

Lori proceeded to bless me with her love and presence, blowing the scent of roses into my face at the very end. When Anna and I walked away from that building and our class, we were on cloud nine feeling very euphoric, yet also a bit cathartic from all the emotional release that happened for us both.

If you met Lori on the street, you would never suspect that she had this incredible way with people. The fact that her touch, her very breath could make people feel differently was quite hard to fathom but I saw it and experienced it with the others around me. It was real, yet like magic!

Later, I purchased some recommended books on flower essences that Lori had utilized also in our class. I continued to study flower essences and trying some out for myself. I was also intensely studying herbs also. This interest has lasted for years and continues now.

About a month later, and after staying up for nights reading *The Mists of Avalon*, I spoke to Lori on the phone telling her my impressions of the book and how I did feel I was living it out while reading the words. In my mind, I knew it was a fictional account re-envisioned by the author, but it had definitely hit a nerve inside of me. Reading the book, I actually felt like Igraine. Lori said it was because I identified deeply with that mother archetype.

Lori invited me to her place in the country and I brought Anna along. The property had a house with a small original log cabin portion and newer section built on. Inside, it was gorgeous in a French Country rustic way. In the main living area beside the staircase, Lori had an artificial Christmas tree (it was spring) that stood about 8 or 9 feet tall. The tree was decorated with everything that spring reminds us of: colored eggs, bunnies, chicks, a beautiful children's storybook with spring-like illustrations. She stated that she kept it up year round and redecorated it each season. Truly, I wanted to be like Lori and have one of these trees in my house and blow the scent of roses from my breath.

I could tell that Lori's husband was very loving and supportive in his role. He bragged on her, even sharing with us during our discussions that Lori's yoni also held these same beautiful flower fragrances. They both referred to the female and male genitalia in eastern terms as they both had studied tantric sex and were proponents of it.

When I watched them together and with their children, I could see what a healthy family dynamic looked like. Their children all seemed engaged with helping or playing and very polite – extremely cool younger beings. The house had a feel to it that seemed like family and home with a big dash of beautiful. Lori had birthed her most recent child at home with a midwife and her husband.

Before Anna and I left that day, Lori again gave us the flower therapy treatment by blowing into our faces. I watched her hands carefully for a vial or something she could be using to make this happen. I saw nothing. I am not sure if you ate flowers you could reproduce the effect. Plus, with her mind, she could instantly change the scent of the flower she was blowing on you. She had changed from roses to lilies while blowing into my face.

During our friendly mentoring sessions, Lori spoke to me about a concept called rebirthing. Her eyes lit up when she explained the process. She insisted that I was ripe and ready for a rebirthing and instructed me on ways to achieve this. This is a spiritual process that involves washing away the old you and rebirthing the new you. It is very much like the ritual of baptism. Rebirthing can happen more than once and can be used when going through any major life change.

If not for the Camelot dream and my insistence on solving a riddle, I would never have met this lady. Yet, I came to realize later that this was just a first revealing of my connection with the Camelot theme. Regarding Lori's ability to blow the floral scents, I believe it to be real. Unable to explain how it works, it appears to be a rare gift.

In one of my flower essence books, roses are described as fully perfected biological entities that were formed by angelic forces. They assist in connecting us with spirit. Even hybrid roses contain this perfected state.

The odor of sanctity is a classic phenomenon that has occurred with many saints. For reasons defying our knowledge of science, these human bodies do not decompose or decay and often produce a sweet odor. St. Bernadette whose visions of the Virgin Mary in Lourdes is one example of this miracle of incorruptibility. Having died in 1879 and her grave exhumed in 1909, eyewitnesses reported her as being very intact with not the least trace of foul odor. Her body is now kept in a glass coffin in France and viewed by many people each year. She is described to look like a young girl sleeping.

There are many more stories of saints who have displayed this sweet fragrance after death along with very limited decomposition including St. Andrew, the monk St. Charbel and St. Teresa of Avila.

Some people experience the strong noticeable smell of roses when none are present. This is reported all over the world. Often, this is attributed to angels and religious figures such as the Virgin Mary or Jesus. Often, people refer to it as the smell of the Holy Spirit. This phenomenon is also unexplained scientifically.

There is lightness in those that walk closer to the spirit of God. They do not worry about what is around the corner. Emitting love in a continuous stream, they exude a calm, peaceful confidence that defies the term magnetism. Perhaps, they defy many of the natural laws of this world. I saw Lori as this kind of person.

How could St. Germain be one of my guides and also hers? Anita Moorjani, who had a very compelling near death experience, says that we can call on a person, guide, or entity at the same time because they have the ability in that realm to simultaneously be with many of us in an unlimited way. Many people who have experienced near death confirm this as well. Additionally, this is known in many esoteric philosophies to be valid within their teachings.

I took to Lori like a bear takes to honey. As she mentored and taught me, I later realized she was just one dimension in my life of rebuilding Camelot. There were others yet to come.

Dreams

"Your longing for me is my message to you, all your attempts to reach me, are in reality my attempts to reach you"
~ Jalaluddin Rumi

Ten years before I met my husband, I wrote this poem in a journal while sitting outside at a local park:

>Where are you?
>Oh man of equal wisdom.
>Are you yet searching for
>The lady that will make you feel as one?
>Come closer, for I am nearing ready.
>
>But why do I call you,
>When you are already here?
>It is that you are faceless and nameless
>Yet your spirit has touched me.
>I have my proof, you see
>Planted in my faith of this illusion.
>
>At the moment in which we physically meet,
>I'm sure that I will know it.
>For your familiar spirit will awaken
>And stir my sleeping love.
>And that wondrous moment could only be
>Part and particle of what I've drawn from above.

This writing was coming from that other place inside me that already knew my relationship with Nathan would not work out. Coming across the journal, I read the poem again so many years later and recognized it was directly from a wiser part of me that I was accessing. There was a seed within me that knew I would recognize my soul mate when I finally met him in this third dimensional reality.

My daydreams involved how to get further ahead and make more money. My occasional night dreams were very interesting. One dream, in particular, was worth writing down.

I'm not sure when the following dream occurred, but it was sometime after I began therapy. My vivid dream placed me at a house and I knew that it was mine. No other person was present in this dream. The house was very spacious with beautiful views of a lake or water from the windows on the southeast side. There were also many evergreen trees. It was definitely a dream home and an idyllic location.

I remember going into the lower level of the house that had an exercise area and a closet that held my toys from childhood. In real life, those toys were long gone. I walked the property and felt like I was really there, experiencing it all. I write this book now from my home which is very much like this. In fact, it is almost identical.

Early in my relationship with Nathan, I dreamed I was living in early America in a log cabin. It was wartime. A man appeared that I was having a secret relationship with. He had stopped in from the war. We kissed and hugged in a small room. For some reason, he wanted to feed me steak.

Nathan was there, but he was injured and laid up in a bed in the next room. I did not want to hurt his feelings but I was so enthralled with my secret lover who looked very much like the man I am married to now and did not know then. When I first met my husband, he continually wanted to grill steaks with me. This dream almost felt like peeking into another lifetime we may have had together.

Over the next year, I began dating again. This was a big step for me after a decade long relationship with Nathan. My dog determined he did not like the first guy instantly when he came to pick me up. By the middle of the date, I knew my dog was right. The second guy was unstable financially and had personal grooming issues. There was no third guy. I just decided to focus on myself and give up on having a relationship.

Honestly inside of me, I wanted to partner with someone who I felt would be my true soul mate. I found a twin soul crystal and purchased it. I dedicated it to that purpose, put it in my room and then sort of forgot about it.

As a psychiatrist and psychoanalyst, Jung speaks of how many of his patients felt great trepidation in telling their own stories that were beyond coincidence due to fear of being ridiculed. Often, we find synchronicities tied to dreams which people may hold very privately. We find minor events and sometimes intimate, larger ones associated with this phenomenon. It can reveal the darkest times of people and their lighter, happier life events.

There are instances in life where one thing is affected and a corresponding thing experiences the same effect many miles away. In physics, this is called bilocality. Some basic examples of this would be identical twins that are separated by time and distance. When one feels pain, the other can feel it as well. They are connected by some force that is invisible to us, but part of the grand design we function within. Now, it could easily be dismissed that because they are identical twins this occurs. While I would surmise that it is more likely because they share the same physiology, this also happens in other situations.

In fact, when you think of someone you have not heard about for many years, and they contact you either by phone, email or regular mail or perhaps show up at the grocery store next to you, this is indeed a coinciding incidence that followed your thought of them. Did you make them appear in your life with the thought? Did you have the thought because a part of you knew they were going to appear? That is the question we have yet to fully answer. Regardless, the likelihood of this having happened and just calling it a coincidence is what some do. Others know this is much more. It is a synchronicity.

Yet, if we live in a holographic universe, everything we experience is as the One. In this model which has been very well explained by the late Michael Talbot (*Holographic Universe*), we see that we already hold all information. Our task is to learn to access it and when we learn to do this at command, it falls into the realm of psychic phenomena. When we do this by accident or without knowing we are doing it, we see it as synchronicities.

Soul Mates

"Go find yourself first, so you can also find me"
~ Jalaluddin Rumi

Time had been spent on a healing journey and a course correction in my own behavior. I continued delving into self-help books and esoteric studies. As I changed, who I would attract did also. It involves where we resonate – what frequency we are on. As we begin to heal, we attract different people to us. Those that don't fit will fall away either naturally or by some other means. So many months later, I did meet someone. I wasn't expecting it and, ironically, Nathan involuntarily introduced us.

My love story begins on a summer evening in 1994 when Nathan appeared at my house out of the blue. Using his old standby excuse to see our daughter, she was with his mother having some grandparent-grandchild time. Nathan felt the cool reception I gave him. Rarely did I ever get a night to myself. My oldest daughter was spending the night with a friend leaving me child free. I intended to stay home, maybe watch a movie, paint my toenails and read more of my growing library.

I stood at the door, hesitating to let him in. Nathan asked if he could use my home telephone to call his buddy Zach. "Of course" I said. Cell phone use was just coming into society at this time and not very many people actually had a cell phone. He phoned his friend and indicated he would be going over to Zach's house to play some music. He asked if I wanted to come along. For no specific reason, I said okay. Getting together with musicians was something I had not done in quite awhile. We would go as friends, nothing else and he knew that. He called Zach back and asked if it was okay to bring his "ex-old lady".

Once we arrived, we parked and Nathan directed me to the backyard where we found Zach sitting on the deck. He was wearing shorts and I could not help but notice how long and skinny his legs were. I remembered thinking to myself, "Wow, I could never be with a guy whose legs were that skinny. No matter how much weight I lost, my legs would always be thicker than his!"

The three of us headed to the basement area of the house. Zach had music playing from a brand new cd and he asked if we recognized the artist. I immediately said, "Sounds like Pink Floyd." He confirmed it was the group's new album. We had a really good time talking together, all four of us, as Zach had a roommate also. We listened to music, and then paused to play music ourselves.

I had brought a bottle of wine with me from home and my camera. I don't know why I had brought the 35mm camera except that I was going through a heavy picture taking phase. I had set up a small darkroom in my basement and was learning to process my own black and white film.

We all drank quite a bit, going through Zach's wine as well. There was a very brief moment during the visit that Zach's eyes met with mine for just a tad longer than what would be normal in a conversation with someone, but I chose to brush that away. I found him really interesting, but it was not love at first sight.

Impressed how positive he was compared to Nathan, he gave off energy instead of sucking it all up. I liked Zach's attitude and I was surprised he would be friends with Nathan. In the twelve years I had known Nathan, not one of his friends impressed me in any way. I had not expected this meeting to be any different.

For three days after that night, I could not get Zach off my mind. I did not know why. He seemed burned into my brain and I just kept thinking about him. It felt like a strange obsession had developed. I told one of my girlfriends about the intense way I could not stop thinking about him.

On the third night, Zach phoned me. He actually had my phone number in his little black book as an alternative way to get in touch with Nathan. Phoning under the guise of trying to reach Nathan, I told Zach that Nathan did not live with me anymore and had not for quite some time. We spoke for a bit and he inquired about the skincare I sold, saying he had sensitive skin. I offered to send him some free samples and he gave me his mailing address. The samples were mailed the next day.

A few days later, Zach called thanking me for the samples and now wanted to order a particular product. I acted business like and offered to take care of ordering that for him. Toward the end of the conversation, he asked me if I would like to go out to dinner sometime. Since I could not get him out of my head, I said yes.

Even though Nathan and I had long since stopped seeing each other in a romantic way, I knew he would be livid if I was dating one of his friends. Zach and I both kept it secret, as long as we could. Nathan did become a little crazy over things when he discovered it and I ended up having to get a restraining order against him.

Zach introduced me to music he loved and I reciprocated with mine. He told me as I sat on his knee one evening that he believed I was absolutely magical and must be an alchemist of some sort.

Our magnificent period of discovering each other was idyllic. I felt I was reliving a modern day version of *The Mists of Avalon* wherein I was Igraine, born a priestess of Avalon who had been married off to Gorlois (Nathan) who was controlling and abusive. I had strangely fallen in love with Uther (Zach) who would later be crowned King and, together, we would begin setting wheels into motion that became the rebuilding of Camelot. Zach and I were laughingly living out this wild scenario as I would speak of it at times since he had not read the book. We compared the archetypes and enjoyed the fantasy of it all.

Have you ever been so enthralled with someone that almost every song contained a part of them? He had become the music and my personal muse. I wrote him poetic letters and he was very romantic in return. He sent me eleven roses with a card saying I was the twelfth rose. I found that single twelfth rose beside his bed the next time I visited him. He didn't tell me he loved me for awhile. He was just as afraid to fall for me as I was him. But, I saw it in his actions and his eyes. He loved me.

Traveling in his car through the countryside on a sunny beautiful July day, we were transported into a dreamlike state together where time passed too quickly and we felt a secret agitation that we could not make it stand still. We were old enough to know that this great falling together in love would someday pass into something else. The intense excitement would end and a new journey of a more committed love would hopefully begin. And that was frightening to me.

Drenched in a love that felt like swirling in a kaleidoscope of colors, I did not want the feeling to end. I spoke to Zach about this and shed tears that we would lose this incredible in sync love between us. He was wise enough to know it could not go on indefinitely. He assured me that he would always love me.

Zach saw the beauty in me that no one had bothered to notice before, even myself. He knew how to draw it out of me like the deep pore cleansing masque he had ordered from me weeks earlier. When I answered the telephone and he would say my name slowly and with passion, I just melted. The tender way he touched my hand or arm, the way he watched me from afar, showed that he saw my best sides only.

A couple of months into dating, Zach wanted to take me on a three day weekend he would have off and asked me to plan our trip. He gave me a budget and we spent the first night camping out by the river at Mammoth Cave National Park. It was a magical August evening with clear skies and lots of stars. For lack of a proper grill area, Zach drove through the forest piling large rocks into the back of his brand new sports car he had custom ordered. He would later joke about it to his buddies, letting them know how head over heels he was about me to do this.

As the crickets created a wondrous symphony for us, we watched the light from the fire pit he had made and enjoyed a sumptuous dinner of grilled fish, potatoes and asparagus. The stars in the sky and the beautiful moon all seemed to be there just for us. It was as if no one else existed.

Lying in the tent after making love, we heard a rustling outside. Peeking out, we saw a small raccoon nibbling the last bits of fish stuck to the foil from our dinner. We both laughed and Zach noted that I referred to the raccoon as a she instead of a he. He said that meant I had good feelings about being female and that was an honorable thing. I felt the fact that he noticed this meant that he had good feelings about females. This was a vast departure from the way Nathan had been. He detested women really, especially his mother who had been nothing but good to him.

We awoke the next day and headed for a cabin I had reserved at Dale Hollow Lake. There, we grilled steaks and made love in the rocking chair on the back deck, much to the chagrin of our neighbors. Oblivious to the rest of the world, all inhibitions fell away.

After two nights at the lake, we headed to Nashville and I listened to Zach's tales of his band visiting Printer's Alley one night while there. We walked the famous alley which was deserted early on a holiday Monday except for the homeless man who asked Zach for money. I was surprised about how Zach had treated him. He talked to him, asking him how he ended up like this. While it was difficult to understand the man's story, I noted how different this was as a response to being asked for money. Zach wanted to know what happened. "How'd you get like this?" he asked.

Nashville was quiet for this holiday and we visited a bar to duck out of the rain and grab a drink. Later, we strolled through an exclusive store that made elaborate costumes for many different musicians and stars. As night fell, we had dinner and headed back home which was three hours away.

Quiet tears streamed down my cheeks on the drive back home that night, and as much as I tried to disguise that I was crying in the dark car, he noticed. We both hated to be apart from each other for even a day. I would go back to my house and he his. Such closeness we shared, how could we stand being apart? As we pulled into his drive where I had left my vehicle, we sat silent for a few minutes before getting out of the car. I knew right then that I wanted to spend the rest of my life with him. Truly, there is no one I had felt that way about before. Later, we laughed many times that we never saw the cave or went out to the lake on that trip.

One day he went outside to his new car and it wouldn't start. He retreated inside and told his roommate he would need to call the dealership right away for service. He had owned the vehicle a few months, so he was used to driving it. It turned out that he was not pushing the clutch in to start it. He told me that his brain was just jumbled thinking about me all the time. What Zach experienced, I did as well. I was living in a fuzzy cotton candy coated existence and it was hard to keep my mind on making money and normal things people do.

He embraced me and my children and we set up house at his place. As I left the home I had been in for many years now, I felt some fear about relinquishing my life there. But, Nathan had become such a problem that I had to notify the police and actually slept with a borrowed revolver a few nights in case he decided to get crazy. His violent and erratic behavior served as one more incentive to move quickly and totally immerse myself into this new relationship with Zach.

During our dating period and marriage, we continually had times when we were totally in sync with one another, thinking the same thoughts simultaneously. For instance, I would think of a particular food I might like and he would call and say, I was thinking about picking up this or that food for dinner. It would be exactly what I had been thinking of, from the exact same small restaurant. We finished each other's sentences and experienced waves of synchronicities off and on. We were definitely resonating on the same frequency and this continued for years.

In our first few years of marriage, we never spent a night apart. Later, circumstances made that impossible. Zach had two beautiful daughters from a previous marriage who lived in another state. We both traveled to see them, staying with his sister while visiting the entire family in the area. Zach had bought me some earrings which were colored just like my orange fall-like living room walls when he met me. They were cloisonné post earrings shaped like a maple leaf. I lost one of the earrings while on our trip. We searched high and low for it in the guest room we stayed in, never finding the earring. I stripped the bed and looked in the sheets and such. I put the sheets in the washer as we left to go back home.

A year later, Zach traveled back to his sister's house for a family event without me. We missed each other terribly. He called me the next day saying that when he woke up that morning, he felt something between his toes. He reached down and it was my earring. We laughed at how strange this was. His sister said that many people had stayed in the guest room and the sheets had been washed numerous times. He joked and accused me of making this happen, as a way of making sure he didn't forget about me. This was typical, however, for lots of strange little things would happen between us.

Truly, I felt like I had found my soul mate. Not only did we share so much in common which created a true basis of understanding, we also got along so well. The geometry worked: circle intersecting circle. No more days of trying to push a relationship into something it was not and trying to make things that did not fit work.

We also had shared similar life events – a difficult parent, kidnapping, sexual abuse at the hands of a stranger – and our love of music, both being musicians. We each had two girls, one dark haired and one light haired.

I was in a fruitful relationship where I felt cherished and uplifted -- not torn down with words or dishonest deeds. Often, Zach would bring me little gifts that were either something he knew made me happy or would be useful to me. It seemed we both had a constant focus on what we could do to bring the other one joy.

Sexually, I now felt safe and free to experience something deeper, almost divine at times, with my husband. Experiencing a sentimental, deeply loving partner was such a revelation and a dive into love on every level.

The initial feelings of being so madly in love were replaced with a more enduring partnership. We still loved each other, but it was not like we are on a crazy love trip with blinders on for everything else in the world. There is nothing like experiencing those intense days and weeks early in a relationship. You mourn their loss, but you also know they have to pass. You just cannot stay in that state all of the time or you would never get anything done.

Zach supported me in my choice of having a homebirth with a midwife when I became pregnant with our daughter. This time, it was a beautiful supportive pregnancy for me. I safely and successfully gave birth at home surrounded by three midwives and my oldest daughter. Zach caught our daughter as she emerged. It was an intimate and incredible experience.

Later, we became property owners of a densely wooded piece of land where we hoped to build our dream home. It was the first step in rebuilding Camelot for ourselves even if it was an air castle for now. We would often drive out to the land and sit on a fallen tree designated our "thinking log". We would envision where the house would sit and where each room would be within it.

Our partnership was tight and we were able to work cohesively together, often having the same tastes in things and not needing to argue over small issues. This is not to say we never had an argument. Of course, we have had a few. When you spend over twenty years with someone, they go through changes and you do as well. I think you learn to have a compassionate adjustment for the shifting circumstances that life brings. And this can be challenging because you want things to remain as they were – a place that was known and comfortable.

It is important to realize what you really love about a person – their guts -- their true nature. What made you fall in love from the beginning with them is something to hold in your heart's memory and you still see glimpses of it as time progresses between the two of you.

For years, it was difficult to determine who the taker and who the giver was with Zach and I. Obviously, a contest had ensued from our first few dates to see who could please each other the most. Always wanting to give back to each, as much as we felt we were receiving from the other or more. We combined our cherished hopes and dreams into one vision that fueled our actions each day.

Over twenty years later, I am not left lonely and unloved as Nathan said I would be. Such a liar he was.

Alchemy in Action

"Ask, and it shall be given you; seek, and ye shall find; knock, and it shall be opened unto"
~ *Matthew 7:7 The Holy Bible*

Zach was working long hours each day and when our new daughter reached age two, I needed to figure out something to do with myself and my career. I had always wanted to be a writer and I toyed with it writing some short stories and trying to send them to magazines for publication. I had my first windows based computer and access to the internet around this time also. Nothing big happened for me with writing. I did not have the discipline, the space or the time. Something more important was going to happen.

My mother was not encouraging at all. My husband and I both remember a phone conversation in which she said, "You will both be scraping the bottom of the barrel your entire life." Perhaps so, I thought. But at least we will be happy together at the bottom of the barrel instead of miserable and nasty like you. Her statement disturbed both of us. Now that I have raised daughters, I have to marvel at her audacity. Who, with a healthy mind, says this to their children?

One day in a store, I slipped and fell on a patch of water and broke my right thumb trying to catch myself. You would be surprised how one thumb on your dominant hand can take you out of commission to do things for awhile. I was very frustrated and felt like I did not know what I could do to make money. At the height of my frustration, I prayed one evening before bed to be shown what I could do. We had a goal about building our own house and it was going to take more income. Actually, it was going to take a miracle or two.

That night, I had a very vivid dream that I was driving a blue SUV. Inside, I had a briefcase and cell phone. I did not own any of these things at that time. Cell phones were in use, but not that many people had them yet. In the dream, I was selling real estate and I was very happy doing it. I remembered the elation I felt inside the vehicle with my phone riding down roads I had never seen before selling houses. I woke up and knew this dream was a sign. Putting the coffee on early, when Zach awoke I announced to him that I was going to sell real estate. He said, "Great!" and was very encouraging.

The odd thing about this is that I never in my life wanted to sell real estate. Prior to this dream, I abhorred the idea. My mother had sold real estate and I remember how she only got paid when a successful closing happened and there were problems and things falling through. I wanted no part of that and had very jaded ideas about real estate sales. Yet, this vivid dream and how happy I was in it convinced me that I needed to do this. By the end of the day, I was enrolled in real estate school. I was following the lead I had been given. I had learned to trust these extremely intense dreams I received as messages or sign posts on where to go and what to do next.

I began in April of 1997 as a real estate agent. It was not easy at first and discouraging. Sometimes my husband would have to give me a 'you can do it' pep talk. In my heart, I knew I was supposed to do this. But I needed it to come together with more ease. I stuck with it and by the end of the year, I was awarded Rookie of the Year in sales only having actively sold for eight months of that year.

By the end of my second year, I had made more money than I had earned working as a secretary for six or seven years combined. This changed our whole financial world. Our dream of a house was starting to take shape as my husband drew up the design and plans for it each night after work.

Selling real estate was very much full time for me. I took my client's interests seriously and made sure I provided them with the best experience possible. In order to make your telephone ring, you needed to have as many properties listed as possible. I took many expired, hard to sell properties that had been listed with other real estate brokers for months or even years and turned them around with a sold sign.

My system involved analyzing and reassessing what the property's attributes were and determining who it would appeal to. I had at least two berm homes and some homes with strange locations. Many of the houses were dated and the owners were not in a position to sink money into renovations. I also secured the business of an architect who was building in a new subdivision and listed his properties as well.

I put a lot of marketing effort into each property and I also kept a little book in my desk where I would write down a page for each property. Each page would be written as if the event had already happened at a future date that I would determine based upon the time period allowed. For instance, I would write: The property at 1234 Maple Street has sold for a great price and the buyers, sellers and I all left the closing table extremely satisfied with the process.

Each morning, I would read these pages on my properties aloud with enthusiasm. Incredibly, this creative visualization coupled with the task of writing it down worked to produce sale after sale. There was still work involved in selling each one and I put out the effort. It was not just sitting at the desk all day reading and writing these affirmative statements. Some of my sellers were very stuck on their asking prices and it did make negotiations challenging. This was often why those properties had been on the market so long. Yet, my yearly report would show that my listings, on average, sold for more than 97 percent of the asking price.

The time I was taking to visualize these properties being sold and writing it down in my little book as if it had already happened truly paid off. I was utilizing intent, positive affirmations, and creative visualization. This worked despite the fact that I sometimes doubted the results would come through. More than anything, I was keeping my attention focused on the properties and this seemed to fuel things as well.

During the early years of real estate and testing out my little book writing affirmation system, I remember one listing I had that was an historic home. It had been on the market for well over a year prior to me taking the listing. I had one day left of having the property listed and then the sellers were going to pull it from me and go with another agent. I had put a lot of time and money into marketing the property. I figured I would lose out on this one.

On Sunday, the day before the listing expired, I was holding an open house at a completely different kind of property out in the country. A couple showed up and we began talking about their needs. They told me they were really looking for something older with more character. I told them about the house whose listing was about to expire. I arranged to meet them at the property a couple of hours later when the open house was over. We met and they loved it. He came into my office the next day and wrote an offer on the house which was accepted. Why should I have doubted when I have synchronicity on my side?

Another early example was that I sold one of my hard to sell listings – a berm home, by leaving the kitchen on Christmas Eve. I received a phone call from a couple visiting family for the holidays. In the middle of baking cookies, I turned off the oven and told my family I had to go show this house now. It was a long drive to another county and as I made my way to the property, I wondered if I was taking the wrong action. After all, it was Christmas Eve and this was a time for family, but I just had a feeling about it.

Once I arrived and met the couple who had inquired, I found out they were going to be making a move to the area, taking over his father's business nearby. They loved the berm home plus the acreage that came with it. Another accepted offer was acquired and I learned to trust that when I felt I needed to take action, not to hesitate.

As the time approached for my husband and me to build our dream home, our banker informed us we would need an additional twelve thousand dollars in savings to qualify for the construction loan. That was a lot to come up with quickly. In February, I wrote in my little book – "By the end of March 1999, I have made over $12,000 income." This seemed like a tall order to me, but I had to make the attempt to get our construction loan.

Luckily, I represented a buyer and the seller on a property I had listed. It sold for $210,000. At six percent commission, I made $12,600 and we closed before the end of March. We had been able to meet the terms to qualify for the construction loan.

During the building of our home, my husband and I had many fortunate synchronicities. First, I was lucky to strike a deal with the man who owned the property next to us. He lived out of town and needed to sell it. I asked to rent the house from him during the time we were building so we could be close to the project. I negotiated a reduced rent for the size of the home in exchange for repainting the interior and doing some minor repairs. We also agreed that when our home was completed, I would list the house for sale. I felt the home would sell easier with furnishings in it than empty and put it on the market two months before we anticipated moving into our new home. It did sell quickly and we made back everything we had paid in rent from my commission, plus some.

One extremely rainy day, there was a land auction happening down the road from our new home being constructed. I had received a flyer on it that just sort of sat on my desk. For some odd reason, my intuition told me to go. It was raining buckets and I questioned why I was venturing to this auction. Luckily, a tent was set up to shield everyone from the rain. They were selling the land off in large parcel lots. My husband joined me an hour or so later, thinking I was just nuts for spending money on this right now. I was questioning myself as well. Yet, the land was going so cheap at the auction and we ended up purchasing a six acre wooded lot. I put the smallest amount of money I could down and did an owner finance on the remaining portion.

A few weeks later, I decided to put the lot up for sale, asking quite a bit more than the deal I had struck at the auction. A gentleman wrote an offer on it with me and I was thrilled to make a twenty thousand dollar profit, only having held the property a couple of months.

My mother visited our house while under construction. It was only at the framing stage with no exterior or drywall installed yet. She looked at the size of it and the beautiful view and said, "When are you going to sell it? You need to sell it right away. I would get it on the market now." This made both of us feel that we didn't deserve to have a nice house. My husband paid less attention to her statements but still noticed them. They held some weight with me. Increasingly, I tried to ignore her nonsense.

I stayed in real estate for thirteen years, leaving it in 2010. With the housing bubble and problems with credit and the banking system, I found myself primarily handling foreclosure properties for banks and even being asked to counsel homeowners at risk of losing their homes. While I loved to help people, there were many very sad situations surrounding all of this. I decided to step away from real estate.

I now write this book from our dream home – a place that began in a night dream I had a long time ago before I met my husband. It came to fruition years later through help from others, divine intervention and lots of synchronicity. And it is the same house I dreamed about, only better, with the lake and everything I envisioned and more. It is amazing how far you can change things when you pay attention to your hunches, intuition and important dreams.

While it is all just material things that we soon must drop away from, my spiritual life and psychological healing helped clear the way for me to create something different. Healing from my past would possibly be a lifelong process. I knew everything was still not perfect with me, but I had made such significant progress from where I was.

Many times while gardening at my home, I would think of how I would love to spend the next chapter of my life – gardening and writing. I had always been a storyteller. My mother says I could recite many fairy tales such as Goldilocks and the Three Bears at age two or three, never leaving a scene out. By second grade, my teacher wrote in my report card that I had a real flair for writing.

Upon leaving real estate, I began selling items online. One year, I had two different authors order items from me and it sparked that idea in me again. Both prominent authors, I had several books sitting in my own library from one of them. The other author had a television series made of her books that I had watched a few times.

I wondered what these authors' lives were like and how they structured their days with writing. I began thinking again of how I could join and be like them as well. And when you ask, it truly is given. Watch for the synchronicities that appear out of nowhere. Pay attention to your night dreams. Hone your skills at daydreaming. Life responds.

There is a part of us that would like to know our entire path of life. What will happen and what is ahead of us is often such a great mystery. If we tune into our soul or the quantum field around us, we are gifted with insights and cues that take us in one direction or another depending on how we choose to consciously act upon that information. Upon reflection, I surmise that the path of our lives must be somewhat veiled or hidden. Otherwise, we will never experience the full emotional integration of experiences ahead of us.

Often, we are not yet resonating in a place where we are ready to know what experience lies in front of us. We must be experimental learners who go through the actual motions of knowing what we perceive as a real level of life in order to gain the gifts that each situation holds for us.

And let's face the fact that we will experience just about every emotion while in this incarnation: fear, love, hate, anger, joy, elation, grief, loss, loneliness, and more. Remembering it is how we process these emotions and how we respond to the stimuli causing it that is the key to our inner growth and final sustenance as spirits having a human experience. If we look for it, there is a gift within every experience no matter how dire it seems when we are enmeshed within it.

Synchronicities and dreams occur to help us process these happenings in our lives. They can consist of warnings, remembrance, awakenings, grace and more. They are often course correctors that nudge us to take action or give us new insight into our life here as human beings.

Ripples

"Synchronicity is choreographed by a great pervasive intelligence that lies at the heart of nature, and is manifest in each of us through intuitive knowledge."

~ Deepak Chopra

Traveling backward in time to the summer of 2001, my husband and I discussed how we were feeling a great deal of anxiety. We could not put our finger on what was bothering us internally. Our relationship was good. We had our dream home. Everyone's health was okay. However, something was chewing at our inner core and we decided that maybe we just needed a vacation and change of scenery.

We made plans to visit Hilton Head Island, South Carolina and took our youngest daughter along. We drove, stopping overnight in the Smokey Mountains which she enjoyed immensely. While at the sea, we noticed there was nothing but black crows. I had visited this locale many times before and often saw seagulls, but not a beach full of crows. There were tons of them and no other birds in sight each day. It may have been normal to see a few, but not an entire beach littered with crows.

At the same time, my two oldest daughters were in New York. This was late July of 2001. My middle daughter bought me a small replica of the Statute of Liberty at the World Trade Center where she had stood at the top of one of the towers overlooking everything just a little over a month before its demise.

Upon our return from the beach, it was back to business as usual. Still, we had our nagging feeling. While visiting the busy road area where all the malls are in the closest town to us, we noticed the parking lots were full of seagulls. We both remarked and laughed how strange and backward this was. We saw nothing but crows at the beach and now sea gulls in our home state, far from the sea, in store parking lots.

Later, I took the crows to possibly mean that death was coming to our shores. This was my own meaning I gave it and nothing more. My husband describes crows as evil, loud, ravenous, cowardice birds because they never fight alone. They gang up on other birds. Perhaps the seagulls and the crows sought out a change of scenery, just as we had.

On September 11, 2001, my daughter who lived in Manhattan was in Spain on work assignment. My other daughter was safe back at home. My husband and I had been watching the television when it was interrupted to bring us the horror that unfolded live that day. We looked at each other and knew that this was possibly what had been gnawing at us for a couple of months. On some level, we had a nervous feeling that we kept thinking was directly related to us, but it was more to our country and world at large.

I wish our feeling or intuitive side would have shown us more. Indeed, there are some that had precognitive dreams of that day, but perhaps could not relay it all and make sense of it. Our intuition is such a valuable tool. It can guide, forewarn and sometimes even predict. We should look for the strange synchronicities and take note of them, as much as we look forward to the synchronicities that lead to something good.

There is a part of each of us that knows, but is unconscious about that "knowing". Likewise, there is also the collective unconscious which Jung wrote about and explained. Collectively, there was a ripple in the lake of our conscious existence together. Many were forewarned. Some had dreams and nightmares. Some had circumstances arise that prevented them from their demise. Others did not.

We must all try and tune into what the collective unconscious tells us. It speaks through symbols, animals, feelings, dreams and visions. It could be that uneasy feeling we carry for an extended period of time and upon self reflection, do not know why. We must listen, watch, and be the observer.

The Law of One

"True friends are the ones who never leave your heart, even if they leave your life for a while. Even after years apart, you pick up with them right where you left off, and even if they die they're never dead in your heart."

~ Unknown

As mentioned earlier, I lived communally for a time with a group of very loving people who were open hearted and spiritually minded. Their day jobs ranged from engineers, managers, and administrative professionals. They were beautiful souls and I cherish the time we were together. I must specifically speak about Sheila. Truly, I valued her humor, friendship, compassion and words of advice. She is one that I kept in touch with after moving on in life for several years and her daughter babysat my children for a time while I worked a second job in the evenings.

Many of the group have passed on to larger life including Ron who was a prominent radio disc jockey in the area, Dr. Don Elkins, and Carla Rueckert, the main channel for all of us and a very bright, loving, sweet soul. Although older than I, Carla was very young when I spent time with her in the early 1980's, A quiet young woman, when she did speak, it was always something humorous or enlightening. Often, she was encouraging others in our group to serve in channeling and teaching them to do so.

Carla's channeling of what is known as the Ra material was accomplished in deep trance, lying down and without conscious recall of what she was saying. It was primarily only conducted with Don Elkins and Jim McCarty and was physically challenging for her and somewhat draining.

In contrast, our group channeling sessions with Carla were in a sitting, meditative, but conscious state. All channeling sessions of each type were documented on a portable cassette tape recorder. For some reason, I have come into contact with much more channeled material than the average person in my life. A great portion of it has been a rich source of knowledge for me.

Channeling is regarded by many as nonsense or suspicious. Yet, so much of what the entire world embraces and puts their faith into is nothing more than channeled information. Much of the bible is channeled. Many authors can tell you that, at times, something larger than self assists them in putting words down on paper or the computer screen. To be inspired (in spirit) is to touch and make connection with the divine.

Sometime around 2002, I visited a local bookstore and was just perusing the shelves. A book literally jumped out at me. I looked at the cover: *The Children of the Law of One & The Lost Teachings of Atlantis* was the title. This resonated with me and since the book had made its new ownership clear to me, I bought it. I had always felt connected with this civilization recounted by Plato and had even named a room in my home, "the Atlantis Room".

The author was Jon Peniel. I smiled thinking of the pineal gland and its huge role in connecting to the unseen. An American, Jon ends up traveling to a remote area of Tibet at the site of a monastery built prior to the Great Pyramid and prior to Buddhism. There, he spends three years learning about The Law of One which are teachings pre-dating Buddhism and all major religions on our planet.

It was a quick read and I found it encapsulated much of what I believed at a core level about spirituality. Brought to us by those of Atlantis, the main principles are, but not limited to, the oneness that permeates all creation. Everything is one with the God Creation Source. Kindness and unselfish love are also major tenants. I recently read that Edgar Cayce also told an earth history that included the Children of the Law of One from Atlantis.

After reading the book, I excitedly spoke with my daughter on the phone about it and the area of Tibet. She was in New York, working for *National Geographic Adventure* magazine and they had coincidently just published a piece on this "Shangri-La" area of the earth where the monastery was located. Hidden from view for many, many years and nestled in Yarlung Tsangpo Grand Canyon area, there are two giant waterfalls gracing the area that had also been kept secret. A gorgeous area of the earth, one waterfall named Rainbow Falls by the monks and another over 100 feet in height. This area lies north of Mount Everest and is situated in a cold, northern climate. My daughter said she would send me the magazine issue. Synchronicity would have nothing less.

China invaded Tibet in 1949. Occupying it since that time, they claim Tibet is now a part of China and has no individual sovereignty at this time. Over the years, many monks have been killed and thousands of monasteries destroyed. This particular monastery held vast libraries of ancient knowledge that were also destroyed. This destruction occurred in the 1990's to this well hidden area for spiritual living.

I find it odd in our world that we will often go and help those that are under siege and attack. Numerous wars have been fought under the guise of some groups of people suffering under the unlawful takeover or will of another country. It is also true that many times this has been the case, such as with Hitler. Yet it seems no one is concerned about the monks who have been driven from their homes. Nations do not band together to stop the murder, destruction of art, ancient writings and structures. Perhaps, truths lie within the ancient texts and art that they do not want us to know.

By this time, I had been on a spiritual quest for over twenty years. Within those time periods, I would sometimes pull away from it, not because I was bored, more so due to the fact that I would become filled with the information and need time to digest it. Like eating at a large buffet, I would take in so much and then I would need to sit with it for a time and test it out in my world. I would shelve what did not resonate with me or that I could not yet understand, and I would apply what fit.

My intense connection with Jon Peniel's book was something I shared with others close to me. I insisted they had to read it. Telling my sister, "These are my core beliefs about spirituality encapsulated in this book." The Law of One he spoke of had not been brought fully into our world until this book. The teachings had remained as hidden as the monastery in the mountains. Obviously, this was part of Jon's purpose to make this information available to others.

Thirteen years later in 2015, I subscribed to Gaia TV. I was watching a show called Wisdom Teachings by David Wilcock. Much of what he spoke of I knew and many things I did not, especially some of the science related data. I noticed a couple of times while watching the show that he had mentioned the law of one. I assumed he was talking about this book I had purchased at the bookstore on the lost teachings of Atlantis – the one I felt closely matched my inner core beliefs.

On a particular episode, he again spoke of the law of one and he mentioned names of people I had been associated with more than thirty years ago -- Carla Rueckert and Don Elkins. He stated that he had lived with Carla for a time and the channeled material was now referred to as the "Law of One" yet also known as the Ra Teachings.

I was blown away. What a coincidence that he was talking about what I had been a small part of in the early 1980's. I had never referred to the material as Ra or the Law of One. We simply called it UFO meditation, a nickname given to it early on. Further, Jon Peniel had not yet written his book on the law of one until many years after the Ra channeling had been named as such.

I began searching on the internet for contact information for Carla and Jim McCarty, her husband. I knew Don had died back in the late 1980's because Sheila had told me about it one day when she came to visit. I came across a website for Carla and associates and e-mailed them.

I received a response from Jim at L/L Research which stands for Love & Light. I was heartbroken to find out that Carla had just passed into larger life and Sheila went a couple of years before her, passing peacefully in her sleep from no known cause. Carla had been challenged since childhood with particular physical situations and some of them had become worse. It seemed that I had let too many years pass by and I grieved for a couple of days not being able to see either of these ladies again.

I was astounded to see that the information that the trio of Jim, Carla and Don had channeled had been turned into several sequential books. Included also was the first early book and many others with the additional channeled material which more closely resembled the work we were doing together at the house where I lived. A small group in a midsize city in America and now the information on The Law of One was going worldwide and being translated into so many different languages.

I did not speak with Jim again for awhile. I heard from him later in the year saying they had started up the meditations again and I was invited to join them, which I did for awhile.

Without watching David Wilcock's Wisdom Teachings, I probably would never have reunited with this group. As I told them at my first meeting, explaining to them about the whole Wilcock thing and the Jon Peniel book, I feel like the Law of One has been tracking me down, finding me my entire adult life.

In the early days, I was the youngest member of the meditation group and not as mature. I remember relating this to them at different times. They would laugh and say, "You are already an adept. You are just remembering who you really are." or something to that effect. I didn't understand totally what they meant at that time. Thirty years later, I do not consider myself a novice, but certainly not an adept. I am always learning and I am always reconnecting with the great God Source of All That Is.

Words that have become labels like "adept" can often play into our human egos in a negative fashion. It implies a better than – less than scenario which is unfair and self serving. While the correct usage of the word adept would be and is totally acceptable, I feel that careful observation of one's self must be utilized to determine the "why" of its use. Do we need a label at all?

Often, my past religious teachings would make me fearful of the channeling process. Indeed, you can attract entities of a negative polarity. Yet, my friends in my circle held no fear. It was all treated matter of fact. I was taught that whenever I felt fear from any source to love it away and to send love and light in that direction from a pure intent.

Carla was a Christian and attended her church faithfully until health prevented it in later years. She felt very close and in tune with the Holy Spirit of Jesus Christ and also channeled a beautiful series of writings she ascribed to this. I realize that many people who are Christians would have some difficulty in understanding how Carla could channel entities from other dimensions and be a part of their faith. She did not see any conflict within it.

I believe it is very important to always use discernment where all information is concerned, especially of a spiritual nature. Within our being, we know what rings true for us and we can listen, test and use reason. We have two hemispheres connected in our brain for a reason and they both have value. We may also come up against fears that have been placed in our subconscious that have no real validity. Sorting this out is part of the discernment process.

Another synchronicity occurred within all of this. Carla passed away on April 1, 2015. I did not know Carla was gone because I had not watched the David Wilcock show yet to even be prompted to try and find her. I awoke around 4 am on April 5th, four days after her death. It was Easter Sunday and I had all of these thoughts coming into my head. I sat down in the kitchen with my laptop and typed for at least a couple of hours. The writing all felt like it was coming from somewhere else. Indeed, it was being channeled and the words flowed so fast I could barely get them typed fast enough.

Many days, I would sit and do my normal writing in a notebook and soon, here would come the download with more information that I had to write as fast as I could. Soon, I had filled up numerous notebooks. I organized all the papers into a binder by chapter subjects. Those writings may be in a book in the future. Secretly, I wondered if Carla was involved in the orchestration of all this happening in 2015. Could she be nudging me to keep working to accomplish something that needed to be expressed?

I am not yet sure of how the Ra Material is connected entirely with me or to what depth. I just follow the signs along my path that lead me to where I will eventually be able to look back and see why certain connections were being made. Synchronicities such as this are the crumbs I follow.

The Law of One is not a religion and should never be treated as such. It is a teaching full of planetary history, concepts for living and progressing on a spiritual path. It is not for everyone. It is one teaching out of a vast sea of knowledge available to us. There are many paths to the top of the mountain. Each of us carves our own way. Our world is a multi-faceted gem that has many sides that all can shine brilliantly. I respect the free will choice of others to explore their connection to Source – or none at all.

I also learned that Carla had created a blog online that was named *The Camelot Journal*. Her husband, Jim, has since taken it over. I asked Jim recently what the connection was and he said that Carla had always felt a pull toward Camelot and had named a farm they owned Avalon. She also was very fond of *The Mists of Avalon* book which was published, of course, well after Carla and I knew each other. In our early years, Carla never mentioned her infatuation with Camelot, nor had I experienced my "rebuilding Camelot" dream yet. That happened a few years later.

Almost finished with this writing, I began reading the memoir of Colette Baron-Reid, one of my favorite people. In the book, she also relates her feelings of connection to the Arthurian time period. It seems I run into all kinds of people that feel this connection to Camelot. Indeed, the Arthurian legend strikes a deep chord in many.

It felt as if things were coming full circle from the early beginnings of my exposure to channeling with my UFO meditation friends. There was not a total sense of finality, but a further exploration to embark upon within myself and my relationship to The Law of One.

Bonds of Blood

"The intuitive mind is a sacred gift and the rational mind its faithful servant. We have created a society that honors the servant and has forgotten the gift."

~ Albert Einstein

It's strange how we mimic others we have grown up around completely unaware that we are doing it. At times, I am suddenly cognizant that I am sitting at my desk with the same posture – cheek resting on my hand with one finger extended and elbow on the desk. This is the same posture my father often had at his desk. I quickly change positions now that I am aware, wanting to have better posture and less staring off into space with an indentation on my cheek.

Most of us pick up our language dialect from our families and a whole goodie basket of habits. Yet we also know that many traits are not learned from our environment. Passed down through generations in our DNA, I often refer to this as "in the blood". Many believe that extrasensory traits are inherited.

My middle sister and I share strong intuition. When my oldest daughter was pregnant with my first grandchild, I was helping her narrow down some names for the baby. As my daughter and I sat at the kitchen bar having lunch, she would read names from the baby book and I would yeah or nay. We did not know the sex of the baby yet. After more presentation of names, she agreed that she loved two names in particular. So, my daughter had one picked out for a boy and one for a girl.

Later that same day, my middle sister phoned and said she had taken a nap and dreamed of a very cute little boy in our family with the same boy name we had picked out. So the exact day we are selecting the names for a boy and girl, she dreams of this same child who is a boy born months later and with that same name. She had no way of knowing this except through precognitive dreaming – tapping into the field.

When my youngest sister was pregnant, they knew it was going to be a girl. Both parents were quite secretive about the name they had chosen. In fact, a clear decision had not been made and it appeared to be narrowed down to two or three choices. I visited my sister and told her I knew what she was naming the baby. "Oh really?" she said. I told her the two names I could see the child having. Her eyes became enlarged and she looked a bit ticked off, wanting to keep the names secret. Both were the two they were contemplating for her first and middle names.

With all the names there are in the world, we narrowed this down exactly without having any idea what names were being considered or even thinking of current trendy names. How we did this is speculation for some. I would say it is beyond lucky guesses and coincidence.

If you believe in reincarnation and that we are all here playing different parts that we have collectively chosen prior to incarnating on this planet, it may be easier to know ahead of time what another person's name would be in the family mix. Many believe we incarnate within soul groups that stick together and play out different roles with each other to facilitate growth. A person in your soul group that triggers the most reaction from you positively or negatively could have some pact with you on a higher pre-incarnation level that they would serve this purpose for you to grow. These things are mysteries until we pass into the greater life and we see the workings of the tapestry revealed. I must admit I have contemplated these ideas as possible, but I am not married to them.

Regarding the act of receiving small bits of information incoming to this reality in the form of precognition or intuition, we could possibly be experiencing moments of accessing the greater consciousness that bleeds over into other realms. Another way of looking at this is based upon the hypothesis that there is no real linear timeline in the grand multi-verse our souls reside in. In this model, we may access others close to us in our groupings and have a knowing that comes to us in this manner.

Oddly, there was a common denominator or synchronicity here with the two children whose names we intuited. Through the course of family discord and a cutting off or going no contact between various family members, my middle sister who correctly dreamed of my grandson was not permitted to know him after a certain age and never saw his mother (my daughter) again at least to the day of this writing.

I have now fallen into a situation where I will not see my youngest sister or her child whose name I correctly predicted. Could it be that we both knew these children's names because they would hold some emotional impact for us – a foretelling of discord in the future?

We often hear of a mother's intuition with her children. Certainly those bonds of blood are immense. When my youngest daughter suffered a miscarriage, I experienced two synchronicities. First, I had an encounter with a black butterfly that day which was very strange in nature. I felt like the beautiful insect was trying to get my attention as it kept flying toward me. Later in the day, I began having a menstrual period even though I was post menopausal. That same day, my daughter began bleeding and miscarried.

I am so empathic with my immediate family that I often have to remind myself to do shielding techniques to keep from taking on the maladies of others. My husband had a bad tooth that was causing him much pain. He procrastinated in seeing a dentist and it was just becoming worse each day. Soon, I began having a tooth that hurt and my jaw swelled up like it was filled with infection. As soon as he made the decision to pick up the phone and make an appointment with the dentist, my problem subsided for I really did not have a tooth situation. I was just empathically responding to his discomfort. This does not happen all the time, especially if I remember to define my own energy well.

Recently I dreamed my grandson was having some issues at school and confirmed with my daughter the next day that he was in a little trouble and may miss a field trip scheduled for that day. He called me later in the day speaking about the situation and telling me he has been thinking of me a lot. Since he lives several states away, I only see him a few weeks out of the year. I feel very close to him and there is a real soul connection between us. I know he feels the same.

These are just a few examples of how ties to those we are close to can be great enough to allow us to tap into a wisdom that is beyond our rational minds. How do we have this knowing? How does this occur in dream states? Intuition is our inner system that guides us in certain directions, nudging us to make specific decisions without logical reasoning to back it up. Our rational minds are often so busy during our waking life. When we slow down our brain frequency in a dream state, we often allow facts to come through that may not be present in our wakefulness.

All of this can also be accomplished while awake. Slowing ourselves down and being mindful of the current moment is key. Daydreaming, meditating or even engaging in something simple, yet creative, like scrap booking, cooking, washing dishes, sewing, woodworking, and such can put our minds into a more receptive state to receive messages from our higher selves.

Admittedly, I spend so much time in my "busy mind", analyzing things to death, that my intuitive self is often hindered and can only come through in dream states at certain periods of my life. My busyness keeps me from being fully connected with all the wisdom and information I can access. It takes me really being aware of this fact and slowing myself down in order to change the situation and become more receptive in a waking state.

This chapter will now end and this book will pause for a dream like intermission.

An Interlude

★ ★ ★

While writing this book, I had the following dream which I will analyze at the end of its telling in classic Jungian style.

★ ★ ★

In my vivid dream, many guests were arriving at my home for a Thanksgiving dinner that I had not shopped for and was unprepared to create and serve. Most of the guests were family. However, I assured them in my archetypical mother personality not to worry -- I would have this feast prepared for them.

I made a hurried trip to a grocery fussing at two men who were so busy talking to each other that they were blocking the door to enter. I then worried about them being mad at me for scolding them, so I laughed and made a joke of it. "I'm sorry if I am acting like your mother." I told them. In my dream, I am thinking that I was sorry for caring what they think and worrying whether they like me or not.

I next see myself attempting to smoke a turkey outside on a grill. I notice that I have left part of the outer wrapping on the bird and it is now useless. Sure, I could peck around inside, but I am afraid that the heat has caused certain attributes of the packaging to mesh with the poultry meat and ruin it.

Guests are still waiting for dinner and conversing with each other. I wonder if I have even offered them a drink. One asks me where we will eat and I point to a room off the kitchen which instantly boasts a large dining room table set up and prepared. Since I had no part in the preparation, I know someone is helping me behind the scenes, but I do not know who they are.

There is a small girl present and she is following me around in my "didn't know I was having a party" mode. She seems to be a part of me and tags along for all my tasks. Soon, there are two more girls.

I decide to take them over to a collection of DVD movies and have them choose something to watch.

Someone asks me if it is okay to roam around and look at the house and all the rooms. I tell them, "Sure, just don't judge me".

I take the three girls next door to a vehicle that I have the keys to but don't recognize it as belonging to me. Somehow, I either own it or have permission to use it. I charge the main first girl with putting the keys in the ignition and turning it on so that we are not running down the battery while they watch the movie in the car. I walk away slowly and watch the girls in the vehicle to make sure they would not try to operate it. As feared, the main girl puts the car in reverse and is attempting to drive it. I quickly run over to the car and turn it off. I fix the vehicle so that they can watch the movie on the battery alone.

Back at my house, the guests are still waiting and I am running around like a chicken with my head cut off, constantly apologizing. At one point, I go through what looks like an emergency exit side door from my house, Contained within this area, there are a few rows of empty stainless steel restaurant style sinks. There are no workers. The lights are out.

I now find myself in my basement and there is an area where quite a bit of water is coming in where the wood meets the stone. I call upon my husband and show him this. He seems very nonchalant about it, just looks at me, and does nothing.

It is pouring rain outside. I walk onto the porch off the kitchen. People are sitting on the wet furniture but they don't seem to care. I had warned them, but they sat regardless. I am in full "mother mode".

My house in the dream sits on a body of water and there are many boats, most of them identical in size and style. Suddenly, a huge white horse the size of a large stallion is galloping down the wooden dock area, rearing on its hind legs with its rider astride. Suddenly, the horse and rider jump into deep water. A fairly good size boat is coming into the dock at the same time and I worry about it colliding with the horse and rider in the water. As I run to the dock area, I look and there is no collision. All is well with the boat, horse and rider.

I look at the water and boats and wonder why I have not taken one out before as it looks so relaxing. The dream ends.

★ ★ ★

The day I had this dream, I had been quite concerned with whether to mention certain life happenings. I did not want anyone getting hurt and I also felt very vulnerable and subject to judgment.

As a writer, you spend a lot of time feeling like you are working on something that is in progress and not "done" like the turkey. I left some of the packaging on the turkey to hide part of the bird. Unsure of fully exposing all the things I had held in the past as shameful or embarrassing, this book had set on my computer approximately seventy percent complete. Now, I found myself immobilized to move forward with all my fears swirling around in my head. Yet, the dream is telling me that if I leave part of the wrapping or covering on this bird, it will be ruined.

It is common for writers to question whether or not they are prepared for the task of putting together an entire book. We can often run behind real or self-imposed timelines. Yet, everyone was waiting on me to serve up the dinner and make it my best. Still, the urgency of dinner was constantly looming in the dream.

I had some help behind the scenes even though I did not know the source. Obviously, I have had much guidance from beyond with the writing of this memoir.

The main girl who was following me represented my inner child. The other two girls possibly represented my two sisters. I wanted to sit them somewhere, away from the adults, and show them a happy, entertaining movie. When the main girl (my inner child) tried to take control of the vehicle (me), I stopped her by limiting what she could do. Yet, I cannot stop my inner child from speaking out. It is part of her healing.

The main feelings in the dream are trying to please too many people at once and being in archetypical mother personality. Codependent feelings show up in my worrying of whether I was too harsh with the guys at the grocery blocking the door and many other ways.

My husband not being roused to take care of a potentially harmful situation with the water reminds me that I am afraid we are drowning and he does not know what to do to stop the leaking.

Someone asks to look around my house and I say fine, but don't judge me. Having perused the many hallways, rooms, nooks and crannies of my house now, you know things about me from this book that most do not. I was the mother who advised her children never to write anything they didn't want on the front page of a newspaper. And here I was about to reveal it all.

The horse and rider plunging into the water at the end of the dream represent me again, risking criticism. Making a huge splash and worrying about colliding with an oncoming boat into the dock area, I find I land safely. I bob back up unscathed. Looking around at all the boats, I wonder why I haven't let loose and done this before? Why did I wait so long to tell this story?

Loss of Control

"Even cowards can endure hardship;
only the brave can endure suspense."
~ Mignon McLaughlin

From the beginning, Zach and I made a terrific team. Together, we tackled many things that were challenging without argument. My weaknesses were his strengths and vice versa. We fit together well. However, life was about to get more bumpy than we had experienced thus far.

Before closing my real estate office in 2010, Zach and I had been getting back into our music. We had so many musicians audition or jam with us that it would be impossible to keep count. Some we formed a band with and others not. We were older now and playing a mixed genre of classic and alternative rock cover tunes. Occasionally, we slipped a little country or pop into our sets, depending upon the venue we were playing. This was a lot of fun for us, something on our bucket list to try and do once more before we could do it no longer. There was no money in it. Of course, we were paid but it never outweighed the time we put in or the equipment costs.

A couple of years into our band, Zach started complaining about pain he was having, saying he had blood in his stool. He kept ignoring it until he developed a large fistula. He finally saw a doctor. I went with him and stayed inside the room for the examination. The look on the doctor's face during the exam let me know this was something to be highly concerned about. I could tell the doctor was trying not to show emotion, but I picked up on it heavily. He recommended my husband have a colonoscopy scheduled as soon as possible.

I had this horrible feeling come over me and I told Zach I had to go out to the car. It was February and the cold air hit my face along with my tears. I felt so bad for him because I knew from the doctor's expression this was very serious. I wiped my face and went back to the waiting room trying to look normal so I didn't worry him.

Within a week, we proceeded through the colonoscopy. While Zach was still incoherent and lying in front of me in the recovery area, his surgeon stepped into the room and also had that grim look the initial doctor had displayed. He showed me a couple of photos he took of the interior rectum and colon where Zach had a fairly large tumor. The doctor said it was probably cancerous. He would know for sure when he received the biopsy results. This began our journey through cancer.

I spent the entire spring and summer taking him to the cancer center for treatment including each weekday during weeks of radiation. Our money was dwindling and I was fighting to keep our dream home and not lose it to foreclosure.

All the things I did prior had long come to an end such as private horse riding lessons for our daughter, shopping trips for clothes, vacations, birthday celebrations. I could easily live without those things, but I did not want to lose our property to the bank. I did not want to watch us go down like I had seen so many others during this debacle of the economy.

My stress level was at an all time high with the constant threat of being in the street and trying to take care of the man I loved as he tried to heal from Stage 3 cancer. And he changed. His appearance changed as he went from being a muscular man to one that literally looked like he was on death's door during chemotherapy.

My poor husband! He had been required to swallow much of his pride as I took care of him in ways now that he never expected a few months earlier. Not wanting to feel like a burden, he often did not ask for the help he needed. Realizing that, I tried to stay tuned into him and anticipate what that might be. I was in overly mothering mode with him, our daughter and completely stressed out on how to make all of these bills work out.

Being around medical personnel almost daily now and knowing I had to pull together a career change since real estate had taken such a dive, I enrolled in college which I had never been able to attend earlier in life. I was able to qualify for a grant that paid for all my tuition and books if I chose certain career paths. I chose nursing and would begin classes in the fall and that was perfect timing as Zach's treatments would come to an end just prior to this.

Cancer took everything away from us that was fun. We lost our band, food lifestyle, sleep, work life, intimacy and, at times, our sanity. It is the uncertainty that pokes at you in the middle of the night, waking you to the fact that you are not in control. You cannot and you will not know everything the future holds. Your fears can rule you at this juncture if you allow them to. And for me, sometimes they did.

Yet, I kept an eye out for the synchronicities. While I know they occurred with many things to help guide me through this time, I did not write them down. Feeling stuck in a dungeon emotionally and not wanting my concern to show, I plowed through, trying to be the strong one for us all. I felt shocked and sick at the way our former joy had been sucked out of us.

I never knew if cancer was going to take Zach but I did not want to say that in front of him. I did not want him to think for one second that I thought he might die. But others knew I feared it. I remember telling his oncologist that we would not do another round of chemo because I knew he would not survive it. He agreed.

I scrimped on money for basic things to be able to buy expensive herbs and supplements to help build Zach's immune system back. I read everything I could find on alternative treatment and therapies. Finding a Reiki Master, I was initiated and attuned by her. I used it on him but did not know if it helped or not. I was beginning to get a glimpse of what it was like to live with complete uncertainty.

Going back in time of what our life was like before the cancer, I have to honestly see that it was not a well pruned rose garden. There were signs that all was not healthy. I was not paying attention to them. Always, our outer world reflects our inner thoughts and emotions.

At home prior to the cancer diagnosis, things were different between my husband and I. Weeds had been growing in the garden of our relationship for awhile and no one was taking a hoe and getting rid of them. I often spoke to Zach about my garden analogy and that we needed to spend some quality time together. He would always agree. Yet, he seemed too preoccupied to engage and do something to make things different. On the few occasions when I encouraged him to go out to dinner with me or have a special alone time, it was like he wanted it all to end as quickly as possible so he could get back to what he really wanted to do. And he did that alone.

We all have patterns we have developed – habits that keep us doing the same thing over and over without variation. Some people seem to have a harder time making changes and Zach showed that from when we first were together. I remember I had rearranged the living room furniture and thought he would be surprised and like it. He didn't. It really seemed to upset his world. He liked everything to stay the same, even if it wasn't the best way it could be.

Zach had a side job selling video games online in addition to his regular work. In my opinion, it consumed him in an addictive way. While at home, it was like he wasn't there. Our daughter and I both experienced it and this had actually begun way before he was diagnosed with cancer. Much of the time, he was actually busy photographing and putting his games online, or perhaps packing an order. Yet there were many days and nights he sat glued to a video game he was playing in his small office alone.

He seemed disinterested in being a part of the family and engaging in a genuine way. He stayed for hours in front of his computer or video game. Intimacy was rare. When I would try to initiate, he seemed agitated at times and welcoming at other instances. I felt lonely a lot even though he was in the same house with me.

During the time we had our band, it gave us something in common that we loved and did together. I took care of doing all the background work such as trying to find other players, gigs, songs, etc. There were many instances when the band would be waiting for him to get off his computer in his office so we could rehearse. He just seemed so immersed in his endeavors.

If I said anything to him about it he became very irate and defensive, telling me it was to make money. I understood that because I sold things online too, but he was spending almost every waking moment when not working outside the home fooling around with video games – either playing them or selling. It seemed obsessive.

His father had passed on just prior to this period and I noticed the change in Zach's personality quite significantly shortly thereafter. I would speak with him about his feelings and he shared that he had a lot of guilt about not traveling to see his father prior to his death.

We did enjoy some fun times together, especially with the band. A nagging feeling played in the background of something being wrong, yet difficult to put your finger on exactly what it was. When the cancer diagnosis came along, it gave my husband something else to focus on. It gave all of us a real concern that had to be addressed.

Following all of his medical treatments, Zach's test in the fall showed him to be cancer free with no spreading and the tumor gone. This was fantastic news and he had begun working again. Often, I felt bad that he had to work, yet a part of him also seemed to want to.

Secretly, I felt like he should be more excited about life now that he was cancer free. I would tell him stories or tidbits of information to encourage this including how lucky he was to be healed from it. I cannot say he didn't feel good about surviving cancer, but often his words which reflected his thoughts betrayed a real show of gratitude.

Since he seemed so emotionally cut off from me, I had burning questions about whether people are even meant to stay married for long periods of time. Perhaps, I thought, people come together and serve each other a certain period of time and then move on. I did love Zach very much. I just wanted us to be close again and there was a wall that I could not break through.

It's the strange silence that falls upon a relationship wherein you know there are things that need to be talked about, but no one does. Whatever the "it" is that begs for light grows in a fertile darkness of repression. Pushed down, these weeds later emerge and before you know it, they are overtaking your previously fruitful garden.

Embryonic Darkness

"Do what you love and the money will follow."
~ Marsha Sinetar

After leaving real estate, I ran my own internet business at home and was now attending college too. Having forgotten anything I originally half-way learned about algebra, they had placed me in pre-algebra during my first semester. I would have to take a lot of math classes to catch up. English was very enjoyable to me and not something I had to spend as much time on. Anatomy and physiology captured my interest in an intense way as I pressed on toward the nursing degree.

Mathematics was a subject I tried to approach with "I can do this" excitement and it often turned into pure hatred. I can say that an excellent teacher is often the difference and since many mathematics professors are not very good at actually teaching, I often did not pair well with them for the task.

English and writing were my favorite classes and I took an additional class in these subjects each semester as electives. During my creative writing class, my professor wrote on a story that I handed in "Absolutely noteworthy and publishable". This really gave me confidence to take my writing more serious.

Sometime during my third semester, I came upon a fork in the road. I was beginning to feel resistance to the idea of being a nurse. Why in the hell was I doing this? I had spent months around the healthcare industry each day with Zach. I had thought about the steady regular pay nurses earn. It was just about the money. My decision was made out of fear of losing Zach and not being able to pay my bills without a regular income since real estate was still down and not coming back up for air yet.

Now in Algebra II Trigonometry, my professor was really lousy. Each class lasted two and a half hours and was situated after lunch. I could barely stay awake with his boring ways. I have never been so unexcited about anything in my life. This was a five hour credit class and required. It looked like from my test results I would be lucky to get a D and I could fail entirely.

Yet, every once in awhile, I would see correlations within math that prompted my mind to think deeply about how the world works. Synchronicity can be seen within mathematical principles. Two angles that fit together perfectly are said to 'coincide'. They are not a coincidence but are part of a design aligning in some way. And I see this intelligent touch of things coming together perfectly all the time. Even when it does not seem like they are lining up to fit together initially, they somehow do.

In the meantime, I was attending advanced anatomy and physiology and these classes were much harder than the 102 course I could have taken. The lectures were long in length, yet extremely condensed due to the vast amount of content to be covered. Again, another five hour credit course with time split between class and lab.

The lab professor was also very spotty in actual hands on instruction. He spent the majority of lab talking about his children. He announced he would not be at our next lab exam because he would be in Disney World with his family. We would have a substitute set in for the test. We did not have many tests in this class so each one counted heavily.

The test consisted of questions printed out on black and white photocopies. All answers were essay style. One section of the test had to do with anomalies in the blood. It would have been very helpful if it was in color so we could tell what we were looking at. I skipped that section and worked ahead on the next one so that I could come back to it and try to make heads or tails of it. There were only thirteen essay questions on the test so each one counted quite a bit for scoring.

As I returned to the section on blood, my own began to boil. I was just livid that he put out this shoddy test while he gallivanted off to Disney World. And it was not just that section. The entire test was poorly photocopied and difficult to read. It was imperative to me that I made a good grade or I might as well kiss being a nurse good bye. I might be able to skate through math on poor grades, but that was questionable too. I had to have "A"s in English and anatomy and physiology or I would not make it.

I sat in my class chair thinking about the entire situation. I hated math. I loved English. I was not good at math, but good at writing. I loved anatomy and physiology, but not the pace we were keeping in this class and the way the instructor sort of dumped us. I was going to be forced to take flu shots and other immunizations every year or I would be fired from my job as a nurse. That didn't set well with me.

I tried to decipher the black and white poorly photocopied blood slides as well as I could and gave it my best. I then wrote on the front of the test – "I'm done with this class. This is the most poorly put together test I have ever seen. You could have at least made the blood section in color copies so we can tell what we are looking at". I got up, turned it into the substitute and left with mixed feelings.

There was a part of me that did not quit at anything and I had that nagging word on my mind: "quitter". I try to never be rude but I wanted the instructor to know how I felt about that test. I ran into other classmates the next day at school who informed me that they felt the same way too and were very concerned about their grade.

My instructor contacted me a week later and asked me to come in and talk. I told him my difficulty in taking the test as it was presented and that I knew I wasn't alone. He stated that it could have been better and would grade it on a curve. I told him I was not really sure about the nursing career. Right now, I felt like I had spent months nursing my husband and what I really wanted to do was write. He spoke about how my knowledge gained in the classes could be helpful relating that Michael Crichton (*Andromeda Strain, Jurassic Park, and ER*) had been a physician originally. That seemed a little pie in the sky to think of the level of that particular famous author, but I understood my instructor's point.

He signed the paperwork for me to withdraw from the class and I came home and told my husband I was going to be a writer. Zach was so totally supportive and always has been. He tells me constantly that he believes in me and I often wonder if he knows how much of a crapshoot it is to make a decent living at this endeavor.

Going back to school allowed me the mental space to come to the conclusions I reached regarding my life, happiness and what I wanted to do. It became more about a true inner fulfillment rather than a job to make money. While money is necessary and I had now experienced what it was like to live on very little of it, I knew that it would ultimately not fix things. I also felt such resistance to the idea of nursing because it would put my empathic nature on overload. So many people suffering in front of me could trigger anxiety inside me that I could not shield myself from. And the rules of it all would bother me as I had such a very holistic approach to my own personal healthcare.

I decided to adopt the philosophy of "do what you love and the money will follow." Learning is lifelong. College is something I could go back to, one or two classes at a time, taking what I want. It is luxurious to think this way but learning at my own pace and without the pressure of a degree felt right to me. I know this sounds unproductive or even irresponsible to some but I wanted to absorb the information and apply it somehow, not just be propelled to quickly memorize and receive a grade for it.

Striking out and telling people you are going to write for a living is foolhardy to your confidence level. Now, I entered a period of even more uncertainty. You can write book after book but if no one buys them, you won't make any money to live. I didn't care. I felt it was in me and part of my purpose. Further, Zach was behind it all the way and was my fiercest cheerleader. He was willing to work and try to make most of the bills while I ventured into this new world.

My style of writing was to be developed through practice each day and this is still the case now. I am in a state of constantly becoming and not often sure what that will look like on the other side once it is accomplished. Writing each morning became a habit. Often, it was just venting. At times, something revealing or relishing popped up on the paper. It was hit and miss and without structure. In a strange way, this made it easy and authentic as I was beginning to transform.

I entered my own cocoon – a state of embryonic darkness. Unsure of what to write about, most of what I had poured out in those morning pages was my feelings. Many days, they were dark and ugly and I look back knowing it was healthy to get it out. There were moments of true love and gratitude too. This is the stage where many people quit with their art. Feeling disjointed and things not working, they give up entirely. Encouraged by Zach and my daughters, I forged ahead but it was slow.

Overall, I still lived in a state of uncertainty about being an author until I realized I just needed to claim that by doing it and being it. I gravitated toward writing something that felt safe, a book on internet business and it was published in 2015.

I held an idea for a fictional series for years – even prior to committing to being an author. Ideas filled a couple of files on my computer and hand written notes in a binder for this storyline that I would write 'someday'. However, something nagged at me in a more forceful way, begging to be told.

It began by thinking of all the incredible synchronicities that have occurred. And it took me on a journey to see how each synchronicity you read in this book fits inside a puzzle. That puzzle shows patterns of behavior and living. It revealed why I did things and chose people in my life that I interacted with. All was there. It was like looking at a piano keyboard. The white keys were the situations, people and decisions. The black keys were the synchronicities that occurred in between. And you have been hearing my song.

Yet all songs end and I found myself completely perplexed on how to end a story that was not yet complete. Blinded, I was inside a story that was stuck in a thick fog and could not see the other side. Directionless, I spent considerable time trying to know which way to go with the remainder of my life. What should my focus be with my marriage, children, grandchildren and extended family? What new calamity would happen as our reality seemed to bring one piece of bad news after another?

Pluto's Punch

"I don't believe in astrology; I'm a Sagittarius and we're skeptical."
~ Arthur C. Clarke

This book began to take shape in January of 2016. However, it has been coming alive my whole life. During this period of writing and prior, I have experienced a time of deep inner transformation on every level imaginable. Almost every facet of my life has been tested.

Going back in time to tell my story forced me to look at it from new perspectives. Often, old hurts that I thought were gone presented themselves once again. I saw patterns – many of them scattered throughout of how I kept replaying an old story within myself and it was often manifesting instantly right in front of me.

Patterns and habits of behavior came to an ugly head during 2017. I was angry at my husband's addictions and habits of living. Yet, if I was honest and looked at myself, I was playing out the same old patterns myself. I thought of the book EQ in which the author speaks of people being stuck at a certain emotional age and never growing further. I definitely saw my husband stuck at the age of a teen at times, unable to express himself very well when he felt emotional other than being angry or sarcastically vindictive. Yet, it was even further back for me. I was often stuck at the young girl stage that felt trapped, could not break free from abuse or what I perceived as wrongdoings. I was not in my own personal power as a woman.

People really will continue to play into the movie you are rolling in your brain if you don't change your thinking. I needed to make a radical change but I was not sure where to start. I saw that all the mothering I was doing was to keep things on an even keel at home and prevent upset. If I take care of this problem or that, then all will be well – except me. I was overdoing constantly and carried way too much burden upon my own shoulders. I seemed unable to let things go and let things be.

I feared everything would fall apart if I didn't "handle" it. Yet, my world continued to degrade and I along with it. I harbored resentment and anger at everyone I felt put me in this position. Yet, it was I who was showing up and volunteering for the job.

I also went through a very restrictive period financially compared to what I had experienced before in my career. This did not last for months, it went on for years and it was time to break free of it for good. All movement toward good seemed to be thwarted at this time and I did not know why.

I would still have some days where at the bottom of everything, I felt unworthy and that I might disappoint others. I would avoid conversations, situations and even things I needed to take care of – my responsibilities. Indulging in self-sabotage, I would unconsciously prove to myself that I was just a screw up.

The cognitive realization of this was revealing but not completely healing. I would need to continue digging deeper into myself and what my thoughts were that I was holding. What new things would I need to learn? I was slipping back into those old patterns. What was triggering it? Was it the writing of this book?

While writing, I had to revisit in as much detail as I could the past and it made me sad inside to know that I had gone astray so many times. Then, I would bounce back looking at great things that had been created. I just wanted to be my best self. The trick was how to balance that because I did not want to let anyone down, including myself. Learning to manage those emotions to avoid slipping into a black sea of feeling not good enough hung over me often.

All of my previous success at writing things down in my little wish book, using creative visualization, meditating and such were not working. I felt jinxed. Something was not right and I needed concrete answers so I could try and fix it.

Visiting my old friend, astrology, I found that Pluto had been transiting my first house in my natal chart since 2008. The first house in your chart rules the outer personality and ego. Pluto, being furthest from the sun, moves slowly and affects a particular sign for many years. Transiting my first house of my natal birth chart was something that most people never have to experience in a lifetime due to the slow movement. Lucky me!

Astrologically, Pluto represents transformation and rebirth. It accomplishes these tasks by totally taking down all things standing in its way. For me, this was creating a complete destruction and reconstruction of who I believed I was and the rebirthing of a new dimension of my real self – that part of me that was coming from my spirit. Indeed, Pluto was punching my ego right in the face and not letting anything progress until I surrendered.

Additionally, Saturn was transiting my twelfth house and it seemed as if even the stars were shaping me into something, but I did not know what. Saturn is always a teacher. As it transited the last house of my natal chart, it was forcing a new maturity upon me to let go of all that needed to leave.

For those of you who are astrologers or follow the subject, you understand these aspects as very cathartic. For those who doubt astrology, I can only say that I see it as the original science of the skies that preceded astronomy. If our own earth's moon affects gravitational pull, ocean tides, human moods, mating practices and women's menses, how can we not be affected by the sun and other planets? As one astrologer put it, the planets and their movements set up a condition – like a weather pattern. We must then adjust our clothing, shelter and choices for living according to the weather.

During this heavy Pluto transit, I had undergone so many changes. My real estate career was over. I had begun and quit college, giving up the idea of nursing. The dream house my husband and I cherished had almost been lost to foreclosure. My husband had stage three cancer and he was spared as well. And there was more to come. It was not finished showing me what I needed to let go of and how I needed to transform.

One year, my personal vehicle worked two months out of twelve despite numerous repairs with different mechanics. This absolutely grounded me at home where I could do little but write and think. I finally had to sell my car I loved for a low price once a small funnel cloud damaged it with tree limbs.

Five and a half years after my husband's tests showed no cancer in his body, he began having trouble getting his breath at times. Finally, I observed Zach barely able to take the kitchen garbage out and begged him to see a doctor. We had spoken about it many times and he had resisted. This time, he agreed and over the next couple of days he was still having trouble with his breath and feeling weak. I convinced him to go to the emergency room with me.

Once there, we were subjected to a battery of tests and he did show elevated levels of troponin which indicated possible heart attack and/or damage. He was admitted and a heart catheter procedure was performed the next day. The results were that he had blockage in all main heart arteries and would require a quadruple bypass.

We found ourselves on a new health journey now with a ton of anxiety hanging over us. Zach's surgery was successful. Bringing him from the hospital many days later, he required oxygen for home use during the first couple of weeks. My daughter and I would raise him from the bed and lie him back down for what seemed like several weeks to avoid his large vertical chest wound from opening or causing pain. My father made him a special chair that put him at a better height to sit at the table so he did not have to bend.

When you go through a bypass surgery such as this, it's a big thing. It is routinely accomplished with a very good success rate but it is huge in scope for what the patient endures. Literature is given to you at the hospital and visits with all the various medical personnel involved are very much wanting patients to take advantage of getting counseling and medication if needed for depression or anxiety. Zach was stuffing his feelings about the experience and secretly resentful that all this was happening to him. It's just not the way he planned his life to be. Yet, he refused any type of counseling and would not even take his pain medication because he did not like how it made him feel.

I took care of him constantly and consistently, letting everything else go. He never cried. The things that would have devastated me seemed not to bother him or at least he didn't show it. He had been so brave about the entire process and surgery. I knew he was not doing well emotionally at times. We had one chair that suited him best in the living room and he would often sit there watching television. Preparing food for him in the kitchen, I could see him from that position and would occasionally notice the foul expressions on his face and a few times they were directed at me.

As time went on and body healing began, he could get around again and finally go a few places. He loved to go to a particular flea market on the weekends looking for video games and I accompanied him not wanting to take a chance of him being there alone. This was on Father's day weekend in 2016. We then picked up take out and went by my parents' home, bringing the food along.

After eating, we sat with my parents and talked. They were repeating stories they had told before as older people sometimes do. I could see that Zach was growing weary of it all and I prepared to leave as soon as the conversation could be nicely interrupted. That seemed to take much longer than Zach was willing to put up with. He became angry, stomping his feet and demanding we leave immediately. He did not feel good. I grabbed things and we made our way home. We left so abruptly and in such a strange way that I was now worried what my parents thought. Being empathic and wanting everyone to be happy, I tried to get out of there gracefully for Zach. Subsequently, I felt our abrupt departure must have left my parents wondering. Silence fell over the vehicle as I drove and he became completely unhinged when I suggested that his behavior was embarrassing to me.

Upon returning home, Zach had an additional outburst that was violent and angry. He turned over a large table on our porch and threw things around. On another occasion, he yelled at our daughter at the gas station when they were pumping gas. It was so embarrassing to her that she said she would never go anywhere with him again. Later, he created a huge argument with her over a delivery fee when we had a pizza delivered. He was moody, giving off a dark energy that permeated the entire house.

Less than two months after quadruple bypass, Zach was having what he described as chest tightness and I again took him to the emergency room. The doctor was not sure what was going on with him but the blood level again showed the troponin levels higher than normal. They admitted him once more and planned another heart catheter the next morning. Zach had a heart attack in the middle of the night that was described as mild, but he was receiving drugs to keep his blood vessels dilated. I was thankful he was at the hospital or this could have been fatal at home without the extra intervention.

The clean arteries that had been taken from his leg to now mend his heart were very blocked – and one almost 100%. How could this be? The doctor who performed the cath procedure looked at me incredulously when he told me of the blockage. He said even if your husband was eating horrible food and smoking, it would take years normally for this to happen. It was an anomaly that no one understood. But, I did. On an emotional level, I suspected that my husband was closed off – to me, his feelings and life.

There was a sadness and grief about all that 2016 had brought to our doorstep. There was guilt for feeling this way because we were lucky – he was alive. Yet, there are many emotions that swirl around such a time in a family and it is during these times when extra love is needed for all.

Stints were put in and Zach was put on more medication to help keep blockages from reoccurring. All of us know our time is limited, but I cannot help but walk around each day with a knowing that his time could happen much quicker.

Over the years, events and the emotions tied to those happenings wore on our relationship. When you look back to try and analyze just what the problem was, there is no single moment or thing. Was it the way you were or he was? Was it the debt we accumulated and then had a hard time repaying, thus money stresses? Was it the health challenges that came our way? For richer or poorer, in sickness and in health, till death do us part is what we vowed. Yet, I often felt like I just wanted off this roller coaster ride.

What about our feelings? What about recapturing our intense love of one another? Why was it fading and why did I often feel like we just cohabitated together? We grew a beautiful botanical garden together but we stopped pulling up the weeds and they were taking over.

The couple that hardly ever had a disagreement began having them with more frequency and often, they were very hurtful. Blame and intolerance of the very things we put up with before in each were now setting in.

Both of us walking around, stuffing our feelings when we did not want to confront the issues. My mistaking his lack of action and prior normal work level for not caring about our family any longer when really, he was very ill with cancer and then heart disease. We just didn't know it then.

Almost everything felt so restrictive without movement toward anything good. I often felt like my hands and feet were bound with invisible tethers. Dragged along with Saturn impacting my twelfth house and Pluto in my first, I could at least now see that these planetary influences were setting up a weather pattern I didn't like. I was going to need to do and be very different. Yet, I did not know how.

What did I need to do different? How did I need to be? Trial and error showed me that it was not something I could just fix like a busted pipe. No, it was something I had to endure and even embrace even though I did not want to. Broke in the pocket and spirit, I surrendered asking God for signs and help.

I learned to allow myself to be shaped by this God force, watching and listening for signs pointing me in other directions. I humbly trusted that there would be a sign, even when there was none. I did not attempt to make it happen. I attempted to let it happen. I adopted the belief that I was always moving toward my highest good even though I was super thirsty many times, walking through a complete desert of isolation with a sandstorm kicking up and unable to see my way. I surrendered to God and let that intelligence be my guide.

There was a sweet freedom in allowing a higher guidance to show me the way. Even when I could not see which way to go, I could sit with that fact and know, believe the direction arrow was coming. Help came in small bits and pieces from spirit. I would catch the right radio or television show with a message I needed to hear at that moment. Complete solutions were not instant. Answers evolved while things still crumbled beneath me.

I learned to live with uncertainty about everything from loved one's health, money, life and death. Not only did I learn to live with it, I embraced it more peacefully without the huge amount of stress like before. Each time I resisted change, I was actually causing myself more stress. I floated in uncertain waters not knowing what shore I would wash upon. Would my husband live and overcome his health challenges? Would I find a way to make money again? I had no answers, but I followed a flow that was just there each day.

With each new challenge, I refused to give up. I was determined to get through this time period. I understood that it must be attempting to mold me for something better, showing me the past that needed to die and the new future awaiting rebirth. Yet each time I tried to grab hold of this silent energy, it would escape through my fingers. There was and there is only one way to get through this type of triple whammy astrological influence and that is a true "let it be" attitude.

I began living without worry more of the time. I began trusting that the house payment would be made one way or another. And it was. Food would be on the table and it was. Those close to me would sometimes shake their head and say, "I don't know how you guys are making it? I don't understand what is going on here?" Sometimes I would regress and there was blaming on my part. I spent time mad at my husband, mad at his illnesses, and angry at myself for even having those thoughts.

Everything did feel like it was coming apart at the seams. Here I was working on a book that maybe no one saw value in and I was unsure of myself. I had other concerns too. After writing approximately half of this book, I became reluctant about publishing, not wanting to make people in my family embarrassed, namely my mother.

I called into psychic Colette Baron-Reid's radio show one day and was very fortunate to get through and be chosen to speak live on the air. She counseled me on the importance of telling my story and to just be true and authentic. Colette saw great things for me with the publication of it. So, I forged ahead with this writing.

Months later, I wanted to call into Colette's show again, hoping I could get more advice now that so much time had transpired since the book's inception. As I dialed the number, I realized they were broadcasting a replay and this was not a live show. I would not be able to ask a question. As synchronicity would have it, the show playing was the same one I had listened to and called into months previous. What are the odds of this happening?

I listened to the entire hour and took notes this time, really hearing myself as the caller and the advice. The message was clear: Tell your story. You have nothing to be ashamed of and stop worrying about reactions from others. Just get the book out there. Realize you don't have to fix everything wrong with yourself to have validity and be a help to others. Where you were is not where you are going.

Other advice included coming to a new self-love and radical acceptance of self. It was stressed to realize I did not have to fix everything that was wrong with me and to cut myself some slack. Colette saw that I would have an understanding of true surrender, not by holding up a white flag, but simply coming to a comfortable acceptance of circumstances.

She said I spent most of my time in archetypical mother energy and asked me to try and step more into woman energy, realizing that the cause of everything is the story underneath that I had been holding onto instead of healing. I needed more time and space to heal and I needed to welcome that and make it happen.

Gifted as Colette is, she intuited all of this without me telling her much about me at all. She stressed that the only way to transform the story underneath was through self love. She reminded me to realize that my mother had her own wounds, hated herself and simply projected that onto me. Bottom line advice was to own my story and tell it.

So, months later the answers were the same about all situations. And I had spent time delving into the past in the writing of this memoir, looking at all my little nooks and crannies and trying to clean them up. I had new respect and love for my perfectly imperfect self but still needed to expand on this. I was learning to float with the uncertainty instead of controlling everything. Yet, I still played the mother role way too much.

Weaning

"As empaths, we are not here to be sponges or enablers. We are here to be helpers, guides and supporters."

--Aletheia Luna, *Awakened Empath: The Ultimate Guide to Emotional, Psychological and Spiritual Healing*

Late in 2016, I received a message psychically to sit on this book and not publish it yet. I felt impatient with that information and thought about going against it a couple of times but acquiesced.

Breaking down how I was spending each day, how many hours were spent on me and how many on others? How had I been an exceptional businesswoman just a few years ago and now everyone's caretaker? My oldest daughter said, "Mom, this isn't like you."

The year had brought such health challenges to Zach and emotional riffs in our relationship. I longed to get away. I wanted to see my oldest daughter and grandson in Florida and I wanted to stay somewhere on the beach. Almost every day, I would daydream about this and fantasize about sitting on the beach and hearing the ocean waves as I closed my eyes.

In November of that year, my middle daughter called and said that unbeknownst to her she had accumulated vacation time that she had to take now or lose. Her boyfriend could not get off work and she wanted to know if I would like to go to Florida with her for a few days by ourselves and also spend a few days with her sister and my grandson. Of course, I said yes. It was a dream coming true for me when I really did not have the resources to do so.

My daughter who so generously took me on this trip did not know I had been fantasizing about such an event. We had never spoken about it. Notice, however, what I said earlier. I would daydream about this a lot. I cannot say I did each day. Yet, I can tell you that I did many days. I kept a calendar in my office with photos of ocean and beach scenes. I imagined the sunshine, sand, sunrises, sunsets, sounds, birds, and more. I saw myself happy and at peace.

It gave me a week to really look at my transformation progress and analyze things. I had not completely healed from codependency and wondered how much I had regressed in some ways. Things felt so out of my control. I had to be there with my husband to take care of him after surgery and had wanted to be. I had to help my youngest daughter with her pregnancy. Those relationship bonds were important. With love, I wanted to help. The emotional outbursts and rage after my husband's surgery were quite a tumultuous time with me thinking we were going to have to go our separate ways. This triggered in me everything that was disgusting and deplorable – behavior I could not be around or live with. Yet, it did pass.

I was heavily into the mothering archetype. It was the dominant theme coming through all my actions and it leaned toward an unhealthy state of codependency. How could I find the real inner me when I was so busy trying to assist and fix everyone else around me? Neglecting the other sides of myself and not feeding myself first was wearing me down mentally, physically and spiritually.

Years ago, my mother had another child after my infant sister who died. Born approximately nine months after my own first daughter, we each had babies that would grow and play together as companions.

But my young baby sister was sometimes mean spirited and showed this from an early time in her development. She often hurt my little girl by hitting, kicking and biting her. She would dig her fingernails into her arms as well. This seemed to be her natural "go to" reaction if she saw a toy she wanted that perhaps my child was playing with. Instead of negotiating or sharing, it was war and domination.

This baby sister also looked more like my mother than my middle sister and I. As she grew, she displayed increasingly abusive tendencies. During her teen years, she was often uncontrollable. My parents told me on a few occasions that they feared she might kill them in their sleep. She became involved in fights at school, yelling and cussing at anyone who even looked at her sideways.

Smart at figuring people out quickly, my sister could be so charming and used that talent on different family members for sympathy, as well as boys. At a certain point prior to her turning eighteen, my parents considered giving custody of her to the state. As much trouble as she was, I felt sorry for her and volunteered to let her come live with me. Luckily, that did not happen. I'm sure she would have turned my world upside down with intense drama. Instead my parents put her into a girls' home for awhile.

We rejoiced at the birth of another grandson on New Year's Eve of 2016 and as this new baby filled our family with love, I had to say goodbye permanently to my youngest sister. She had blown into town from another state for the holidays and created such havoc within the family that it became intolerable to continue any relationship with her.

She verbally attacked me behind my back conducting a full blown smear campaign of lies. Worse, she started doing the same with my grown children. I had to institute a no-contact policy with her. This was all unprovoked in any way by me or my grown children. In fact, I had gone out of my way to be so nice to her since I rarely see her.

Angry for days, I finally began to look at my sister's actions as a gift to us. Her perplexing antics compelled me to get on the computer and try to find an answer to this outrageous behavior. Why did she conduct a smear campaign against me and tell all those lies? Why did she try to pit or triangulate her two sisters against each other? Why did she run to our parents and make up lies about my children (their grandchildren) to them?

After spending days reading voraciously and listening to experts speak about malignant narcissistic and borderline personality disorders, it was obvious that my youngest sister had both and our mother could as well. Very little was known about these two disorders when I underwent therapy. Plus, no one could get my mother in front of a therapist long enough to diagnose her.

All those years of dad blaming my mother's behavior on hormones were now explained. Both my mother and youngest sister had conditions that made them different in a way that was not ideal, but at least was now identified.

This freed me in such an enormous way. I realized there was a small part of me that was still frightened of my mother and people like her. Secretly, I had wanted them to like me and I wanted a relevant, deep relationship with both my mom and youngest sister. Now, I had reached the Rhett Butler moment of not giving a damn. I realized that nothing I could ever do would keep them from undermining or attacking me because they had a deficit inside their brains.

For years, we had known there is "something wrong with mom" and had looked for answers high and low. Some in the family would say, "Well, she runs either hot or cold". Her children knew the extent of her abuse which was physical and verbal – always psychological. She would make you out to be the crazy one if you told anyone what she was doing.

My sister closest in age to me said she often caught my mother talking to herself in the mirror, mostly like she was having a confrontation with someone else with an entire dialogue. She said mother never even seemed to know she was there in the room, observing her. She also might carry on these conversations with herself while washing dishes. If you asked who she was talking to or "what did you say", she would snap and say she had said nothing.

Recently, my mother stated emphatically that "people are who they think they are." She said this twice in the same conversation. From the perspective of a narcissist, this is true. They never get down to a core level of who they really are. They have to wear masks and they feel their value is reflected in those around them.

The fact that these incidents never happened when my father was at home told me that my mother did have some degree of control over her emotional outbursts. Yet this is common for people with personality disorders of which my mother suffered.

People with these conditions have actual differences in their brain structure. This causes them to view their world differently and react in ways most people would not consider. You could be completely innocent of something and they will build a complex case against you just because they've decided you are their enemy to be destroyed. This is what I experienced with my youngest sister. Without her having done this, I may never have gained an understanding of what was going on with my mom. Suffering from borderline and narcissistic personality disorders, she has been the difficult sister to be close to.

A new compassion came over me knowing that neither of these ladies could totally help who they are. At this time, there is no cure for these disorders. There is one psychological treatment being explored to help. Yet, I believe we must also shield and protect ourselves from people who may do us harm. It is absolutely necessary to have strong boundaries with people suffering Cluster B disorders and sometimes, cutting off all contact with them is the only answer.

This was not the first time I had been subjected to my sister doing these things. Since she had moved to another state and I did not see her much, I was free from much of her drama for the last few years. When I saw the potential damage she could do in just a short time during her visit, I decided that no contact with her was best for me.

This all weighed heavily on me in January of 2017. The over mothering archetype went into full force as I felt I needed to protect myself, my grown children and this new baby grandson. I definitely had my own problems and patterns that needed to be resolved. Yet, they set into a tighter pattern that was crazy and not liberating.

I found myself taking over the care of the baby grandson because my daughter lived with us. This would happen because I was afraid she either would not step up to the plate the way I thought she should or perhaps out of my need to be needed. Plus, I loved the little guy. But, I took it too far and forgot about myself.

By May of 2017, I was completely worn out with childcare. In the meantime my daughter was out in the work world, going shopping, leading a normal life. I was neglecting myself, still in my robe many afternoons and not showered. This is what new mothers endure and I had already "done my time" with my own children. It all began to feel so out of balance. Yet, I constantly held the idea that if I did not do it, who would? Would they do it right, i.e., as well as I can do it?

If I am an experienced farmer and a young couple buys the farm next to my land and I see that they need help because they know nothing about farming. I then take it upon myself to go over and show and tell with them all the aspects of farming. Later, I go out to their fields and start tilling, plowing and planting for them. As weeds grow, I take care of that for them also. Then comes the harvest and knowing just when to pick the fruits of their (my) labor. You see, they learn very little to nothing this way. Instead, my own fields are now neglected because I have spent all my time taking care of their farm. I could have just lovingly said to them, I am here if you have questions or need assistance or advice.

And that is what I was doing with my baby grandson. I was so afraid my daughter would not or could not handle her new motherhood that I found it easier to take over for her, yet it was creating a situation that compounded things because she needed to do all the little things that new mothers must do to take care of their young. I sat up a situation in which I turned her and my grandchild into major life projects. I was also teaching her that the only way she could accept her new position and be happy with it was by getting me to do what she did not want or feel like doing at the time.

Was I avoiding who I really was – what I am here on this planet to accomplish or do? Perhaps, I needed to look at this more closely than what I perceived their neediness to be. Perhaps I needed to reconcile within myself that I was in a pattern of needing to be needed because there were aspects of me that I did not want to deal with. And, as much as I was not allowing them to grow, their acceptance of my overbearing motherly help was not allowing me to grow either.

And it was the same for my relationships with my youngest sister and mother. As long as I continued to play into their versions of reality and not move myself away from it, I was hindering them and myself from any potential progress. My point was not to punish my sister by going no contact. It was for preservation of self. Perhaps someday we could reunite. With my mother, I kept contact open but extremely limited. I would see if we could coexist in this manner and time would tell.

The Living Nightmare

"As Above, So Below"
~ adapted from *The Emerald Tablets of Thoth*

In early November of 2017, I made a genuine attempt to straighten up my office and begin the task of clearing my writing area and trying to figure out how I would have the space and time to publish my memoir and participate fully in its launch. I had not worked on my writing for four months! Glancing to the left of my writing area, I saw that my wall calendar was stuck on the month of June, the date when all my plans began to blow up.

Sunday, June 25th of 2017, I had arrived home from visiting my parents with my grandson in tow. As I placed him in his high chair in the kitchen, I walked a few steps to turn on the light and noticed a lot of dirt on the switch plate. As I looked closer, the dirt was moving. It was moving, but slowly. I knew my husband would be home soon so I would leave it there for a few minutes for him to see and get his opinion on what it was. Once he arrived, he immediately said it might be bird lice.

Less than a week prior, I had been sitting on the screen porch off the kitchen. I kept hearing the high pitched sound of baby birds and had told my husband that it sounded like there was a bird's nest with babies under the screen porch. He investigated as the mother bird eyed him with great agitation. Sure enough, there was a nest with babies and he decided to leave it until the young ones had flown the nest.

Wow, if we had only known! Oh my, our world completely changed. Within a day of the baby birds leaving the nest, bird mites invaded our home. So tiny in size, ten of them could fit through a regular hole in a screen. They looked like tiny dots of pepper. We are not sure of their entry point but they were all over the light switch and we feared they were in the wall.

We found that regular Windex killed them on contact and after cleaning all of them that we could see, we assumed we were safe. Browsing the internet, we read of horror stories of homes infested with bird mites and how it was worse than bed bugs. We read of people who battled them for months and some for years. With false confidence, we thought those people must not know how to clean and get rid of things.

A few nights later, I awoke to a horrid, creepy feeling. There was a crawling sensation on my body from my feet and lower legs that was slowly rising up my body. I got up and turned on the light and could see nothing. I took a shower and stayed up rather than getting back into bed.

I experienced this several nights with the mites actually crawling into one of my eyes, going for my ears and mouth, and yes, they will even try for your private parts. The mites are looking for moisture. They only ingest blood from mammals and if there is no bird or rodent host, they will go after humans.

I had small bite marks all over my body within a week or two and each time one would bite, it did hurt. It is a quick pinprick bite that is sharp and distinct.

Although the mites first went after me and everyone in the house thought maybe I was imagining this, they soon attacked my husband and our baby grandson as well. Our daughter was not affected by them and, with research, we learned this is common. They will find their favorites.

I spent my days and nights washing walls, clothing, bedding, floors, furniture, counters, and vacuuming over and over again. Cleaning the same things repetitively like spring cleaning was each day of the week.

Carpets, tile and wood floors were steamed. Pesticides were put down. Everything we owned was put in heavy plastic bags for protection because these little suckers like to hide in cottony fabrics when not using you as a snack.

Worst of all, we unknowingly spread them to someone else. And, you won't believe who! Yes, it spread to my mother's house. We are not sure how. She and my father visited us once briefly in July and I visited her with my grandson once in August.

The mite situation cost us a ton of money, physical energy and sleep. We could not see family for Thanksgiving. I could not see much of my family at Christmas. And people did not want to see us. Who could take the chance?

Earlier in the year, I had worried what I would do if my youngest sister came to town for the Christmas holidays. Would I just opt out and not attend dinner at my parents' home? I really had no solution. Since my parents and I both had these mites, that solved the dilemma.

At one point, I wanted to just get in the car and leave our home. There was only one problem with that as I realized something very insidious. They were now in my body. I went to the doctor. I collected them and got an initial lab analysis but it was not correct. It took an entomologist to identify exactly what creature we were dealing with.

I slept very little and actually became afraid to go to sleep in my bed. Our couches and chairs were treated and sealed up. Our mattresses and box springs were completely sealed with thick contractor grade plastic. Nothing was worn or used more than once. If something dropped on the floor, we assumed it could have a mite on it and back into the laundry cycle it would go. I did laundry 18 hours a day, every day. The water company called us twice to report that we may have a water line break due to high usage.

My washer broke twice, the dryer once. While waiting for repair, this was my only downtime from laundry. The amount of housework I did everyday was enough for a team to take on, much less one person. This combined with caring for my grandson often felt like it was going to physically do me in.

I found out through the family grapevine that my youngest sister, that I was now estranged from, had experienced bird mites at her home a year or two prior. She began offering up advice (through that same grapevine) of how to rid ourselves of them. Her solutions had already been put into practice and were helping, but not totally eradicating them. She lived several states away and there was no way she brought this on us. We know what the source was – the nest that my husband removed with one dead baby bird in it. It was covered in bird mites that immediately got all over his disposable gloved hands.

By the time I had to call everyone and confirm that I would not be hosting Thanksgiving dinner, I just had to laugh at the absurdity that I saw in all of this – an absolutely strange synchronicity. Bird mites! Such an obscure problem to have that most people may never encounter. Who did encounter it? Me and the two people I had conflict of some sort with in life – a triangle appeared in my mind of me, my mother and my sister.

With the intense mother archetype I had been displaying, word play came to mind – nests – nesting – leaving the nest – babies – latching on – parasitic – taking over house – getting under skin – invading – taking up residence. There was a distinct pattern.

Amazingly, there was huge denial in the medical and pest control community. Most of them said this could not happen. Some said bird mites won't even bite humans. Others agreed they may bite but would not burrow into the skin. They were wrong. I knew what I experienced and what I was now seeing with my mother's skin as they had invaded her as well. I felt horrible that this had transferred from my household to hers.

Each time I would apologize about it, she would blame it on my father, saying he was the reason because he was always going to auctions and flea markets picking up used things. She was deflecting to him because she actually did not want me to feel bad. Perhaps behind my back she said otherwise, but at least to me, she was not blaming. She had every reason to pin it on me. I felt a deeper compassion for her than before. I felt like she had grown and I admired her for how she was trying to handle all of it.

This bird mite invasion was so serious. I tried so many things natural and toxic to rid them. There is not one single thing that worked. I would say it was a constant collective effort of using everything at your disposal to rid your body and home of these creatures.

One day I wondered -- what if I loved these little parasites away? What if I did just as I was taught with my Law of One mates back in the 1980s? What if I also felt genuine gratitude toward the mites for the gift they were giving me, for the tremendous catalyst in my life?

The mites were showing me I literally allowed others to suck the blood out of me at times; to feed off my energy in ways I am no longer comfortable with. And the keyword was that I was allowing it. The universe was displaying this in a huge way mirroring this fact with the mites. It was a clear case of "as above, so below". For myself, I knew on a metaphysical level that I had to make a huge leap in consciousness and vibration to co-create a different reality than the one I was experiencing. I had to absolutely be, think and feel differently.

As I delved into what this situation was showing me on a larger level, I attempted to truly express a let it be attitude. I knew that the mites were trying to survive just as much as I was. Once I relaxed into this train of thought for a day, I had something miraculous happen. While standing in my kitchen, I heard a voice that was not mine. It said not to worry; that they were gone from my body and I would never experience that again. I told my husband about the voice and he was encouraged, but probably held some disbelief. Honestly, I had doubt myself. Yet, I knew from my life and past experiences that I should just be open and believe. I never had them in my body again and I don't believe I ever will.

What of the synchronicity triangle of my mom, youngest sister and myself experiencing the mites? They were doing their best to survive with the skill set they had been born with and had acquired. It was the same for all of us – creatures large, small and microscopic. This deepened my compassion and love. Everyone and everything is resonating where it is until it vibrates higher, thus changing its experience.

We can overcome, we can rise above our circumstances no matter how insidious they have become. We can break the patterns that bind us -- the self imposed prisons of our own making. We must love ourselves so much with a real inner knowing that we are meant to birth something wonderful out of something ugly. And this is how we rise people. This is our metamorphosis. The technique is individual for each of us and while the formula is relatively simple, it involves a complex network of thoughts and feelings that have turned into our beliefs that must be examined and determined if real or not.

I knew that as I began to change my overly motherly ways and adopted an attitude of surrender – to let things be – my experience would shift. It began slowly. Each day as I caught myself in the act of doing otherwise, I would quickly do a course correction. And this moved me closer to inner peace and a mite free home.

Epilogue

We can stay in our trauma stories consistently and be miserable. We can do that – it's our right to choose. But, there is a difference in having the right to blame and stay where you are and making the changes necessary to give yourself what you rightfully deserve. We are all going to have times when life does not match what we expected. We all have trauma – what we do on the other side of it is what counts.

Tragedy and challenges will always occur to us and those we love. How we respond to these trying situations defines not only who we are inside, but what direction we will head into.

We have the ability to overcome whatever happens to us by not giving up and making excuses. Almost all of us have good minds that can look and recognize patterns that keep repeating in our lives. We can break free from those invisible tethers and grow into our best selves, relishing our best lives. This results in finding out that we are so much stronger than we thought we were. We also grow stronger emotionally and mentally each time we break through these challenges – becoming more whole each time.

Sometimes, the work is not difficult. You have a moment of grace poured upon you whether you feel you deserve it or not. One day, I experienced in a single moment what many people term an awakened healing. It was as if I had been asleep and suddenly awoke to the idea that I am something different now. I am no longer the woman worried about what people may do to me or how they may react to me. I acknowledged that I had to continue to make a conscious effort to practice self love and taking care of myself in a way that allowed me to be of help to others. Learning that loving me was loving others, I still played mother, but began moving swiftly into grown woman with her own needs too.

I gave myself a new blank slate mentally to be … not someone different, but the true self I felt had been squished between layers of guilt and self loathing. I no longer saw myself as a victim. When I thought momentarily about anyone who had abused me, it was like that situation had become compartmentalized over on a shelf somewhere and I could just let it collect dust. I had read that book and indeed lived it, but I did not need to read it again. The book was a part of my literary repertoire but not my total experience. The knowledge of it had shaped me, even defined much of my life, but that's only because I didn't know about all these other books that contained a new different reality for me to explore if I would just be brave enough to pick them up and begin reading.

So I stood as a human with head on shoulders and heart in the upper torso. Mentally, I imagined pulling who I really was now from my heart and slipping it into all those crevices of my brain. I knew this was the key -- to primarily live from this heart mind, using the knowledge I had stored in my brain for discernment.

I had no reason to fear life or people. Whether they struck me down or just gave me a crappy feeling, I now knew how to get away. I could protect that inner child who had suffered and ran away so long, she knew little else. My fantasies of having a big brother who would be my champion and right the wrongs were no longer needed. I was my own champion and I would now move in a direction to be a champion for others.

Moreover, I held a trust that was so fierce in its composition, an intense knowing that no matter what, I would be guided by watching for the synchronicities and listening to my dreams. There was something greater than I could imagine that would propel me toward my best outcomes even when it would appear I was traveling through stormy skies. Synchronicity was always there, running in the background. It only required that I listen, observe the message, feel the lesson and miracle it held for me to learn, grow and be a better me. This gave me courage.

It is this hope I have for you; that something of value comes through this retelling and that you know you are not alone. You have your own stories and dragons that will rise. Each time, you have the opportunity to confront and transmute it in order to tame it. You have a purpose – a divine one – that is perhaps awaiting its emergence through your own rebirth. We can rebirth ourselves many times throughout one lifetime.

Realizing that I do not need to have everything worked out here at the end of this book in some neat little wrapped up fashion. I am evolving. You, as a cherished reader, are evolving. Our stories are evolving. And I have come to a comfortable level of acceptance of situations, still with knowledge that I need to set boundaries and not slip into my mothering, codependent ways.

I am struck by the fact that everything we have gone through in our human experience is much larger than the event itself. This is not to minimize the feelings we experience during an event we felt was negative, abusive or challenging. It is to open the curtains and look through a metaphorical window that shows us a larger view of why we have endured this happening. This is an individualized process that can only be interpreted through our own psyche. Further, this knowing can come instantaneously or may evolve over time.

So it is apparent that these experiences carve us and we have the option to heal the scars and use that knowledge to assist others to do the same. Growing from these experiences requires us to really go within, looking at our participation in the event. It calls for authenticity coupled with a compassion for the suffering of others, gradually opening those drapes so we can see the light and move forward.

Memoirs are always about what has gone before. When I think about where I see things going in the near or distant future for myself, it is still hazy and mutable yet very pointed in some aspects. The philosophy and ideas contained within The Law of One are very much a part of what humanity can embrace in order to progress to a higher level instead of devolving into a more animalistic nature and fighting each other with sticks and stones – which surely could happen if course correction is not installed.

We are witnessing an extreme amount of upheaval in our societal systems. Old ways of doing things from every realm: medical, financial, political, parenting, education and more, are crumbling. Some desire to return to what they perceive as a more original way of doing things. Some want to turn all of it on its head and have no rules at all.

For me it is very important to be a champion for those that have no power and often cannot speak for themselves. Children must be given better starts in life. Certainly, widespread abuse – verbal, physical, neglect and sexual must be stomped out of the world. I will make a prediction that it will be the mistreatment, harm and even murder of children that will bring all people together toward a common cause. This cause will permeate all income levels and ideologies as masses of people become shockingly aware of the depth of this quiet, yet horrific, problem.

The main thing to focus on for each of us is looking at ourselves. What are the patterns or habits of thinking, being and doing that we use daily in our lives? How do they shape our world? What can we do as one individual to change ourselves, and thereby change the evolving tapestry and our world? How can we give to each other without taking a tremendous toll on ourselves? How can we be loving and also loved?

We can experience the world as quite magical if we do not always rely on science or logic to explain everything. Synchronicities, although we may be unable to pinpoint their cause, do occur along with divine interventions. Forgiveness of self and others is a key component to healing. Knowing that, as much pain as someone may have inflicted, it was also a gift if we choose to see the good that may come from it. And, that can be very difficult to do. Heartfelt gratitude for our lessons propels us even further toward our true purpose and good. When we are confused in darkness and fear, love always knows the right answer.

As I sat down at my desk to wrap up this book and give it to you, I knew with a certainty that reverberated into my bones that I was meant to carry a message. I was meant to reveal my secrets. I was meant to absolve any tiny crevices left of shame. This revealed patterns that could be torn away and made into fresh lay lines that created a new map -- one that had been turned on its axis and was now a sunnier place where I knew how to love myself, love others and feel compassion as intense as any great mother would have for a child. A child who is learning, a child with knowledge veiled that must find her or his bearings in a dimension that is tricky and treacherous at times. And with discovery of self and mastery of same, rides a tamed dragon into a beautiful blue sky.

Be still and look at the starry sky
Know this story goes on without end.
Even when I transpire and ascend,
The story of synchronicity extends
Through iridescent light threads that intersect
We feel the pull toward our highest and best

You are the story and your thread intersects with all the other stories out there. Sometimes, when those threads touch, a synchronicity happens that causes you to pause and think about where you stand and what your purpose is in this universe that seems so vast. It shows you the patterns and the pieces of you that need mending and those that are tumbled and finished, ready to wear like an exotic jewel.

Let your light shine and keep working on those dusty corners of yourself that need love and forgiveness. Know that each of us has such significance and that includes you. Your story is being written now and you are the author. Go make it magnificent. Later, we will stand in awe of the tapestry we created together.

Thank you and if you appreciate my work, I would be honored for you to leave a review on any or all of the major sites. Books with reviews are shown in search results and suggested more by online booksellers who rely heavily on these algorithms. It can be a one word review, a few sentences or paragraphs – whatever feels right for you. Just a few thoughts are very much appreciated!

If you know someone who could benefit from reading this book, please suggest it to them.

Have a question or want to tell me about your synchronicities, thoughts and dreams? I would love to hear from you. Write me at contact@lyraadams.com

See what I'm working on at: www.lyraadams.com

www.ingramcontent.com/pod-product-compliance
Lightning Source LLC
Chambersburg PA
CBHW031414290426
44110CB00011B/377